Knit Your Own
SCOTLAND

JACKIE HOLT & RUTH BAILEY

BLACK & WHITE PUBLISHING

First published 2012
by Black & White Publishing Ltd
29 Ocean Drive, Edinburgh EH6 6JL

3 5 7 9 10 8 6 4 2   12 13 14 15

ISBN: 978 1 84502 505 2

Design by Stuart Polson and
Richard Budd Design
Printed and bound in Poland
www.hussarbooks.pl

Contents

Introduction

Scotland may only be a small country but it's one of the best in the world. With its stunning scenery, epic history, friendly people, and more inventions and innovations than you can shake a shepherd's crook at, Scotland's contribution to the world has been immense.

Now, in *Knit Your Own Scotland*, we present some of our favourite Scottish icons, things that remind us what a great place Scotland is to live in, to work or to visit. Enjoy knitting freedom fighter William Wallace, national bard Robert Burns and tennis hero Andy Murray. There's also Miss Nessie (our glamorous version of the fabulous Loch Ness Monster), a Scotty dog, bagpipes, some very cute sheep and lots more.

With step-by-step instructions and great results, we hope you'll enjoy knitting your own little bit of Scotland as much as we have.

Jackie & Ruth x

www.knityourownscotland.co.uk

You will need

MATERIALS:
Colour Codes:
1 Rowan Fine Tweed Dent
   (Brown shade 373)
2 Rowan Felted Tweed
   (Green shade 158)
3 Rowan Fine Lace
   (Gold shade 00930)
4 Rowan Kidsilk Haze
   (Gold shade 00658)
5 Rowan Pure Wool 4 Ply
   (Rust shade 00457)
6 Sirdar Snuggly DK
   (Brown shade 0200)
7 Rowan Fine Tweed Arncliffe
   (Oatmeal shade 360)
8 Debbie Bliss Baby
   Cashmerino Black
9 Rowan Baby Merino Silk DK
   Shell Pink
10 Hayfield Bonus DK
   (Brown shade 0947)
11 Rowan Fine Lace
   (Green shade 00924)
12 Rowan Kidsilk Haze
   (Ginger shade 00649)

18cm plastic boning
Fine cord
Fine millinery/craft wire
Hot-fix studs
Plasti-Kote Fast-Dry Enamel
in gold leaf
Stuffing
Pastel pencil (blue)

NEEDLES:
Size 10/3.25mm
Size 10/3.25mm double-ended
Crochet hook
Jewellery pliers

William Wallace

More than 700 years after his death, William Wallace's name remains known around the world thanks to his heroic fight for Scottish independence. From a noble Scottish family, Wallace grew up at a time when Scotland went from the peace and stability of the reign of King Alexander III to instability and uncertainty when there was no obvious heir to the throne. This led to King Edward I of England defeating the Scots at the Battle of Dunbar and decisively gaining control of his Scottish neighbours.

William Wallace was a huge, powerful man and played a key role in the uprising against English rule. He continually refused to bow down to King Edward and his reputation as a freedom fighter grew as he used guerilla tactics to attack the English forces. He then joined forces with Andrew Moray and their small Scots army won a famous victory at the Battle of Stirling Bridge, when the narrow crossing over the River Forth prevented the English army from attacking the Scots effectively. After Stirling Bridge, Wallace's reputation was made, but he also became Edward's most wanted man.

The following year, in 1298, a still-furious King Edward sent another army north to quell the Scots. This time, at the Battle of Falkirk, Scots resistance was broken. Wallace managed to escape but his reputation was dented. With the English back in charge, he had no option but to lie low, and he travelled in Europe for the next few years. When he returned to Scotland, Wallace was betrayed and captured by the English. He went on trial for treason in London and, after the guilty verdict, he was hanged, drawn and quartered – a brutal end which made him a Scottish martyr and hero. The Wallace Monument, close to Stirling Bridge, commemorates his life and work and, of course, the Mel Gibson movie *Braveheart* has spread the heroic story of William Wallace around the globe – even if it is as much fiction as fact.

Knit Head, Body Front, Body Back & Arms as per Basic Doll

LEGS

COLOUR 6

- Cast on 20
- 1st row: K
- 2nd row: P
- 3rd row: K
- 4th row: P
- 5th row: K6, K2tog, K1, K2tog, K1, K2tog, K6 (17sts)
- 6th row: P
- 7th row: K5, cast off 7, K4 (10sts)
- 8th row: P – pulling 2x sets of 5sts tog
- Work 4 rows in moss-stitch
- 13th row: in moss-stitch inc in 1st & last (12sts)
- Work 7 rows in moss-stitch
- 21st row: inc in1st & last (14sts)
- Work 2 rows in moss-stitch
- 24th & 25th row: Work in reverse SS
- 26th row: P row – join colour 9
- 27th row: K
- 28th row: P
- 29th row: K row – inc in 1st & last (16sts)
- Work 19 rows
- Cast off

To make up: Sew-up back-leg seam matching colour change. Stuff.

T-SHIRT

COLOUR 7

Double-ended needles
Cast on 46
Working on 4 needles:
Work 22 rows

BACK:
Turn work around

- Cast on 4
- Next row: P27
- Turn:
- Cast on 4
- Next row: K31
- 3rd row: K1, P to last, K1
- 4th row: K
- Repeat rows (3 & 4) 5 times
- Cast off

FRONT:
- Cast on 4
- Next row: P27
- Turn:
- Cast on 4
- Next row: K31
- 3rd row: K1, P to last, K1
- 4th row: K
- 5th row: K1, P to last, K1
- 6th row: K
- 7th row: K1, P to last, K1
- 8th row: K14, sl 1, K1, psso, K15
- 9th row: K1, P11, P2tog, K1 (14sts)
- Turn – working on right-side front:
- 10th row: K
- 11th row: K1, P10, P2tog, K1 (13sts)
- 12th row: K
- 13th row: K1, P9, P2tog, K1 (12sts)
- 14th row: K
- Cast off

WORKING ON LEFT-SIDE FRONT:
- 9th row: K12, sl 1, K1, psso, K1 (14sts)
- 10th row: K1, P to end, K1
- 11th row: K11, sl 1, K1, psso, K1 (13sts)
- 12th row: K1, P to end, K1
- 13th row: K10, sl 1, K1, psso, K1 (12sts)
- 14th row: K1, P to end, K1
- Cast off

To make up: Join shoulder seams, and underarm seams. Create lacing at front of tunic with length of Colour 1 thread. Dress doll.

TUNIC – MAKE TWO PIECES

COLOUR 10

- Cast on 22
- 1st row: K
- 2nd row: K2, P2 – repeat rib to end
- 3rd row: P2, K2 – repeat rib to end
- 4th row: K2, P2 – repeat rib to end
- 5th row: P2, K2 – repeat rib to end
- 6th row: P2, K2 – repeat rib to end
- 7th row: K2, P2 – repeat rib to end
- 8th row: P2, K2 – repeat rib to end
- 9th row: K2, P2 – repeat rib to end
- Repeat rows (2-9) 3 times – total of 25 rows from start
- 26th row: Cast off 4, K1, P2, K2, P2, K2, P2, K2, cast off 4
- Work rows 3-5 on remaining 14sts
- 30th row: P2, K2, cast off 6, K1, P2 – turn:
- Working on 4sts only:
- Work 3 rows: K2, P2
- Work 4 rows: P2, K2
- Cast off
- Join wool to 4sts on other side of neck:
- Work 7 rows in rib pattern as other side of neck
- Cast off

To make up: Join shoulder seams. Join side-seams halfway down. Apply Hot-fix studs to create armour effect. Dress doll after T-shirt & kilt attached.

BELT 1

COLOUR 6

- Cast on 3
- Work i-cord 30cm

This belt used at waist to hold plaid in place.

BELT 2

COLOUR 8
- Cast on 4
- Work i-cord 30cm

Make two small buckles from craft wire. Colour using gold paint. Stitch to ends of belts. Secure to figure. This belt used over shoulder to hold sword.

CORDS FOR GAITERS (X2)

COLOUR 1
- Cast on 2
- Work i-cord 36cm

Bind around legs as per photo

CUFFS (X2)

COLOUR 1
- Cast on 12
- Work 3 rows K
- 4th row: K1, P to last, K1
- 5th row: K
- 6th row: K1, P to last, K1
- 7th row: K
- 8th row: K1, P to last, K1
- Work 3 rows K
- Cast off

To make up: Sew around wrists as per photo.

KILT

COLOUR 1
- Cast on 25
- K 2 rows
- Working in SS, using colour codes:
- Work 4 rows in 1
- Work 2 rows in 2
- Work 4 rows in 1
- Work 2 rows in 3 & 4 together
- Work 6 rows in 1
- Work 2 rows in 5
- Work 4 rows in 1
- Work 2 rows in 6
- Work 4 rows in 1
- Work 2 rows in 2
- Work 6 rows in 1
- Work 2 rows in 3 & 11 together
- Work 6 rows in 1
- Work 2 rows in 5
- Work 4 rows in 1
- Work 2 rows in 6
- Work 6 rows in 1
- Work 2 rows in 2
- Work 4 rows in 1
- Work 2 rows in 3 & 4 together
- Work 6 rows in 1
- Work 2 rows in 5
- Work 4 rows in 1
- Work 2 rows in 6
- Work 4 rows in 1
- Work 2 rows in 2
- Work 6 rows in 1
- Work 2 rows in 3 & 11 together
- Work 6 rows in 1
- Work 2 rows in 5
- Work 4 rows in 1
- Work 2 rows in 6
- Work 6 rows in 1
- Work 2 rows in 2
- Work 4 rows in 1
- Work 2 rows 3 & 4 together
- Work 6 rows in 1
- Work 2 rows in 5
- Work 4 rows in 1
- Work 2 rows in 6
- Work 6 rows in 1
- Work 2 rows in 2
- Work 4 rows in 1
- Work 2 rows in 3 & 11 together
- Work 6 rows in 1
- Work 2 rows in 5
- Work 4 rows in 1
- Work 2 rows in 6
- Work 6 rows in 1
- Work 2 rows in 2

- Work 4 rows in 1
- Work 2 rows in 3 & 4 together
- Work 6 rows in 1
- Work 2 rows in 5
- Work 4 rows in 1
- Work 2 rows in 6
- Work 7 rows in 1
- K 2 rows in 1
- Cast off

To make up:
Using reverse side of SS as right side, darn ends of all colours.
Press flat.
 Pleat 28cm of 'fabric' into a finished length of 17cm. Press pleats in, as per a kilt. Leave remaining 22cm of 'fabric' flat. Sew ribbon along reverse side of pleated section to form a waistband.
 Dress doll with T-shirt.
Add kilt to doll from right-side seam, across front, around the back and fix with waistband ribbon. Remaining fabric to be used as plaid over the shoulder, over the tunic, add stitch to hold in place.

HAIR
- Colour 5
- Cast on 40
- Work 9cm in SS
- Cast off
- Colour 12 – use as double-thread
- Cast on 40
- Work 6cm in SS
- Cast off

To make up:
Steam-press both pieces of knitting. Unpick these to create crinkly wool. Cut into approx. 5-inch lengths and knot onto head using a crochet hook, mixing the two colours as per photo.

TO CREATE FACE

Add eyes and mouth in appropriate colour. Add eyebrows to match hair. Nose is a crocheted chain, doubled-over at end and stitched to face. Colour face with blue pastel pencil.

SWORD

Cut shaped piece of boning for blade and cross-hilt. Join using craft wire. Paint and decorate with hot-fix studs, wire & fine gold cord.

EXTRAS

If you want your William Wallace to be a true Scotsman, you can get a little extra knitting idea by visiting www.knityourownscotland.co.uk Please note, this additional pattern is only for bravehearts!

MATERIALS:
Colour Codes:
1 Rowan Baby Merino Silk DK
Shell Pink
2 SMC Select Extra Soft
Merino Black
3 Sirdar Snuggly DK
(Brown shade 0200)
4 Rowan Fine Lace (shade 00930)
– use double
5 Rowan Felted Tweed
(Green shade 158)
6 Brown Chenille
7 Sirdar Calico DK White
8 Rowan Cotton Glaze
(Green shade 812)

Small buttons (for jacket front)
Small beads (as waistcoat buttons)
Small amount of calico/fine cotton
fabric (for book)
Pastel pencil (red)
Stuffing

NEEDLES:
Size 10/3.25mm
Size 12/2.75mm

Robert Burns

Robert Burns is renowned as the finest poet Scotland has ever produced. Born on 25 January 1759, Robert was the eldest of seven children and his parents were tenant farmers, poor folk who lived a hard life. Robert was fortunate that his father believed in education and he soon began to write poetry, inspired by the very many loves of his life.

By 1786, Robert had had enough of his time in Scotland and decided to emigrate to find a new and more prosperous life. As he was trying to raise the money he needed, it was suggested that he publish a volume of his work. This collection was the famous Kilmarnock Edition and it became an instant success. Suddenly, at the age of 27, the name of Robert Burns was known throughout the land and his plans to venture abroad were put on hold.

The next ten years were spent farming and working as an exciseman but his romantic adventures and his writing continued apace. He produced some of his best work in this period and will forever be remembered for work such as 'Auld Lang Syne', 'To A Mouse', 'Ae Fond Kiss' and 'Tam O'Shanter'. Ill health caught up with him, however, and he died in 1796 at just 37 years of age. The first Burns Supper to celebrate his life and work was held a few years later and now, on Burns Night on 25 January each year, Burns Suppers are held around the world – a fitting tribute to the man known as 'The Bard', who is Scotland's national poet.

My Luve is Like a Red, Red Rose

O my Luve's like a red, red rose
That's newly sprung in June;
O my Luve's like the melodie
That's sweetly play'd in tune.

As fair art thou, my bonnie lass,
So deep in luve am I:
And I will luve thee still, my dear,
Till a' the seas gang dry:
Till a' the seas gang dry, my dear,
And the rocks melt wi' the sun:
I will luve thee still, my dear,
While the sands o' life shall run.

And fare thee well, my only Luve
And fare thee well, a while!
And I will come again, my Luve,
Tho' it were ten thousand mile.

Knit Head, Body Front, Body Back
& Arms as per Basic Doll

LEGS – MAKE TWO

COLOUR 1
Size 10/3.25mm needles
- Cast on 16
- 1st row: K
- 2nd row: P
- 3rd row: K5, K2tog, K2tog, K2tog, K5 (13sts)
- 4th row: P
- 5th row: K3, cast off 7, K2 (6sts)
- 6th row: P pulling 2 sets of 3sts tog
- Work 4 rows SS starting with K row
- 11th row: K1, inc in next, K4, inc in next, K1 (8sts)
- Work 7 rows SS starting with P row
- 19th row: K1, inc in next, K6, inc in next, K1 (10sts)
- 20th row: P
- 21st row: K1, inc in next, K8, inc in next, K1 (12sts)
- Work 7 rows SS starting with P row
- 29th row: K1, inc in next, K10, inc in next, K1 (14sts)
- Work 15 rows SS starting with P row
- Cast off

To make up: Join, stuff and attach to body.

BOOTS – MAKE TWO

COLOUR 2
Size 10/3.25mm needles
- Cast on 22
- 1st row: P
- 2nd row: K
- 3rd row: P
- 4th row: K7, K2tog, K1, K2tog, K1, K2tog, K7 (19sts)
- 5th row: P
- 6th row: K4, cast off 11, K3 (8sts)
- Work 3 rows SS starting with P

- 10th row: K1, inc in next, K4, inc in next, K1 (10sts)
- Work 3 rows SS starting with P
- 14th row: K1, inc in next, K6, inc in next, K1 (12sts)
- Work 3 rows SS starting with P
- 18th row: K1, inc in next, K8, inc in next, K1 (14sts)
- Work 5 rows SS starting with P
- Change colour to brown:
- 24th row: K1, inc in next, K5, inc in next, K5, inc in next, K1 (18sts)
- 25th row: K
- 26th row: K
- Work 8 rows SS starting with P
- Cast off

To make up: Sew boot together around foot & leg.

BREECHES

Use double thread
COLOUR 4
Size 10/3.25mm needles

- -

FOR RIGHT LEG:
- Cast on 18
- Work 10 rows SS starting with K
- 11th row: K1, inc in next, K14, inc in next, K1 (20sts)
- Work 5 rows SS starting with P
- 17th row: K1, inc in next, K16, inc in next, K1 (22sts)
- Work 3 rows SS starting with P
- 21st row: K1, inc in next, K18, inc in next, K1 (24sts)
- Work 7 rows SS starting with P
- 29th row: K1, inc in next, K20, inc in next, K1 (26sts)
- 30th row: P
- 31st row: K
- 32nd row: P
- 33rd row: K row – inc in 14th stitch (27sts)

- 34th row: P
- 35th row: K
- 36th row: cast off 3, P to end (24sts)
- 37th row: cast off 3, K to end (21sts)
- 38th row: P

Put stitches on pin

- -

FOR LEFT LEG:
- Cast on 18
- Repeat rows 1-38
- 39th row: K row (right-side facing) – K20 from left leg, K last st of left leg tog with 1st st of right leg, K 20 (41sts)
- Work 14 rows SS starting with P
- Cast off

To make up: Join inside leg seams. Join crotch. Dress doll.

WAISTCOAT

COLOUR 5
Size 10/3.25mm needles

- -

RIGHT SIDE:
- Cast on 3
- 1st row: K
- 2nd row: P
- 3rd row: K – row, inc 1st & last (5sts)
- 4th row: P
- 5th row: K row, inc 1st st (6sts)
- 6th row: cast on 2, P to end (8sts)

Put work onto pin

- -

LEFT SIDE:
- Cast on 3
- 1st row: K
- 2nd row: P
- 3rd row: K row – inc 1st & last (5sts)
- 4th row: P
- 5th row: K row – cast on 2, K2, K to last st, inc in last st (8sts)

- 6th row: P
- 7th row: cast on 2, K left-side, add right-side to needle – K to end (18sts)
- 8th row: P row – cast on 2, P to end (20sts)
- Work 17 rows SS starting with K row
- 26th row: P2tog, P2tog, P6

TURN – NOW WORKING ON RIGHT SIDE:

- 27th row: K row – inc in 1st, K to last 2, K2tog (8sts)
- 28th row: P2tog, P6 (7sts)
- 29th row: K row – inc in 1st, K to end (8sts)
- 30th row: P
- 31st row: K row- inc in 1st, K to end (9sts)
- 32nd row: P
- 33rd row: K
- 34th row: P row – cast off 3, P to end (6sts)
- Cast off

NOW WORKING ON LEFT SIDE – WITH RIGHT SIDE FACING:

Join thread

- 26th row: K2tog, K2tog, K5, inc in last (9sts)
- 27th row: P to last 2, P2tog (8sts)
- 28th row: K2tog, inc in last (8sts)
- 29th row: P
- 30th row: K, inc in last st (9sts)
- 31st row: P
- 32nd row: K
- 33rd row: P
- 34th row: K row – cast off 3, K to end
- Cast off

To make up: Sew to front of doll. Add beads as buttons.

JACKET

COLOUR 6
Size 10/3.25mm needles

LEFT-BACK TAIL:

- Cast on 7
- Work 4 rows starting with K row
- 5th row: K to last 2 sts, inc in next, K1 (8sts)
- Work 5 rows starting with P row
- 11th row: K to last 2 sts, inc in next, K1 (9sts)
- Work 5 rows starting with P row
- 17th row: K to last 2 sts, inc in next, K1 (10sts)
- Work 3 rows starting with P row
- 21st row: K to last 2 sts, inc in next, K1 (11sts)
- Work 3 rows starting with P row
- 25th row: K to last 2 sts, inc in next, K1 (12sts)
- 26th row: P
- 27th row: K to last 2 sts, inc in next, K1 (13sts)
- 28th row: P
- 29th row: K to last 2 sts, inc in next, K1 (14sts)
- 30th row: P
- Put on pin

RIGHT-BACK TAIL:

- Cast on 7
- Work in SS with 1x K st at beginning and end of each P row, unless otherwise stated.
- Work 4 rows SS starting with K row
- 5th row: K1, inc in next, K to end (8sts)
- Work 5 rows SS starting with P row
- 11th row: K1, inc in next, K to end (9sts)
- Work 5 rows SS starting with P row
- 17th row: K1, inc in next, K to end (10sts)

- Work 3 rows SS starting with P row
- 21st row: K1, inc in next, K to end (11sts)
- Work 3 rows SS starting with P row
- 25th row: K1, inc in next, K to end (12sts)
- 26th row: P
- 27th row: K1, inc in next, K to end (13sts)
- 28th row: P
- 29th row: K1, inc in next, K to end (14sts)
- 30th row: P
- 31st row: cast on 9, K to last 2 sts

Next row: sl 2 sts from the pin of the left tail alternately with the last 2 sts of the right tail – forming an overlap of the two pieces. Ktog the penultimate of the right with the 1st of the left. Ktog the last of the right with the 2nd of the left. K to end (35sts)

MAIN BODY OF JACKET
(continue working with tail-piece)

- Cast on 9 (44sts)
- 1st row: P
- 2nd row: K6, K2tog, K2, K2tog, K20, K2tog, K2, K2tog, K6 (40sts)
- Work 9 rows SS starting with P row
- 12th row: K1, inc in next row, K7, K2tog, K2, K2tog, K10, K2tog, K2, K2tog, K7, inc in next, K1 (38sts)
- 13th row: P
- 14th row: K1, P2, K8 – turn

TO CREATE RIGHT-SIDE FRONT:

- 15th row: P8, K3
- 16th row: K1, P3, K7 – turn
- 17th row: P7, K4
- 18th row: K1, P4, K6 – turn
- 19th row: P6, K5
- 20th row: K1, P5, K5 – turn
- 21st row: P5, K6

- 22nd row: K1, P6, K4 – turn
- 23rd row: P4, K7
- 24th row: K1, P6, K4 – turn
- 25th row: cast off 2, P1, K7
- 26th row: cast off 5, K to end
- 27th row: cast off 2, put 2sts on pin

TO CREATE BACK OF JACKET:
Work on next 16sts
Work 12 rows in SS – without the K st at beg & end of P rows
- 13th row: cast off 4, K8, cast off 4 – put on pin (8sts)

TO CREATE LEFT-SIDE FRONT:
- 14th row: K8, P2, K1 – turn
- 15th row: K3, P8
- 16th row: K7, P3, K1 – turn
- 17th row: K4, P7
- 18th row: K6, P4, K1 – turn
- 19th row: K5, P6
- 20th row: K5, P5, K1 – turn
- 21st row: K6, P5
- 22nd row: K4, P6, K1 – turn
- 23rd row: K7, P4
- 24th row: K4, P6, K1 – turn
- 25th row: K7, P4
- 26th row: cast off 2, K1, P6, K1 – turn
- 27th row: cast off 5, K2, cast off 2 – put on pin

To make up: Join shoulder seams. Add buttons.

COLLAR

Pick up sts on pins:
- 1st row: K2 from right-front, K2 from back, inc in next, K2, inc in next, K2, K2 from left front (14sts)
- 2nd row: P
- 3rd row: K2, inc in next, K8, inc in next, K2 (16sts)
- Work 7 rows SS starting with P row
- Cast off

SLEEVES

COLOUR 7
Size 12/2.75mm needles
- Cast on 18
- 1st row: P
- Change to Colour 6
- Size 10/3.25mm needles
- 2nd row: K1, K2tog – repeat to end (12sts)
- Work 9 rows in SS starting with P row –– without the K st at beg & end of P rows
- 12th row: K1, inc in next, K to last 2sts, inc in next, K1 (14sts)
- Work 8 rows in SS starting with P row
- 21st row: P row – cast off 3, P to end (11sts)
- 22nd row: K row – cast off 3, K to end (8sts)
- Cast off

To make up: Join seam & inset in jacket.

RUFFLE FOR NECK

COLOUR 7
Size 12/2.75mm needles
- Cast on 20
- Work 5 rows SS starting with P row
- 6th row: cast off 18, K2, cast on 2 (4sts)
- 7th row: K row – inc in every st (8sts)
- 8th row: K
- 9th row: P
- 10th row: K2, inc in next, K2, inc in next, K2 (10sts)
- 11th row: P
- 12th row: K2, inc in next, K1, inc in next 2sts, K1, inc in next, K2 (14sts)
- Work 6 rows SS starting with P
- 19th row: P2tog, P2, P2tog, P2, P2tog, P2, P2tog (10sts)
- 20th row: K1, K2tog, K1, K2tog, K1,

K2tog, K1 (7sts)
- Work 3 rows SS starting with P
- Cast off

To make up: Join at front neck. Tuck inside waistcoat.

HAIR

COLOUR 3
Size 10/3.25mm needles
- Cast on 6
- Work in Garter stitch
- Work 2 rows
- 3rd row: inc in 3rd & 4th st (8sts)
- 4th row: K
- 5th row: K2, inc in next, K2, inc in next, K2 (10sts)
- 6th row: K
- 7th row: K2, inc in next, K4, inc in next, K2 (12sts)
- Work 3 rows
- 11th row: cast on 5, K to end (17sts)
- 12th row: cast on 5, K to end (22sts)
- 13th row: K
- 14th row: K1, inc in next, K18, inc in next, K1 (24sts)
- 15th row: K
- 16th row: K, inc in 5th & 20th (26sts)
- 17th row: K
- 18th row: K, inc in 12th & 15th (28sts)
- 19th row: K
- 20th row: K3, K2tog, K18, K2tog, K3 (26sts)
- 21st row: K2tog, K2, K2tog, K1, K2tog, K3, K2tog, K3, K2tog, K1, K2tog, K2, K2tog (19sts)
- 22nd row: K1, K2tog, K1, K2tog, K1, K2tog, K1, K2tog, K1, K2tog, K1, K2tog, K1 (13sts)

- 23rd row: K
- 24th row: K2tog, K1, K2tog, K3, K2tog, K1, K2tog   (9sts)
- 25th row: K2tog, K2tog, K1, K2tog, K2tog (5sts)
- Work 3 rows
- 29th row: K2tog, K1, K2tog (3sts)
- Pull wool through 3sts

To make up: Sew to head.

TO CREATE FACE

Referencing Alexander Nasmyth's famous painting of Burns stitch on face using wool of similar colouring. The nose is a crocheted chain. Rosy-up cheeks with soft pastel pencil in red. What a handsome lad. Mothers, lock up your daughters!

POETRY BOOK

COLOUR 8

Size 11/3.00mm
Create a knitted rectangle 5.5cm x 3.5cm. Fold in half to create book cover. Insert pages created from calico/fine cotton.

You will need

MATERIALS:
Colour Codes:
1 Sirdar Calico DK White
2 Rowan Baby Merino Silk DK Shell
Pink (for body)
3 Anchor Artistic Baby Soft White
Crochet Cotton
4 Cream DK
5 Sublime Cashmere Merino Silk
DK Yellow (shade 0250)
6 Red DK
7 Blue DK – small piece
8 Sirdar Snuggly Snowflake
Chunky White
9 Debbie Bliss Baby
Cashmerino Black

Beads for front of waistcoat
Fine gold twine or cord (for detail
on shoes)
Fine millinery/craft wire
Jewellery pliers
Pastel pencil (red)
Short length of gold braid to edge coat
Stuffing

NEEDLES:
Size 10/3.25mm
Size 10/3.25mm double-ended
Size 11/3.00mm
Size 13/2.25mm
Crochet hook

Bonnie Prince Charlie

When Prince Charles Edward Louis John Casimir Sylvester Severino Maria Stuart was born in Rome in 1720, there were high hopes that he would one day regain the thrones of England and Scotland. As the grandson of the exiled Stuart king James II & VII, the family always believed that it was his birthright and that one day he would be the Catholic king of Great Britain.

After a life of privilege and military training in Rome, Bonnie Prince Charlie was ready to stake his claim, and in 1745 he set off for Scotland. His Jacobite cause had support from many of the Highland clans and he raised his standard at Glenfinnan and assembled an army big enough to march on Edinburgh and take the city. Bonnie Prince Charlie and the Stuarts were back and when they defeated the government army at the Battle of Prestonpans, the whole country lay at his feet.

He then headed south and at Derby, just over 100 miles from London, the army stopped and the decision was taken to turn back, against the Prince's better judgement. A strong rumour of a government force massing further south led to this turnaround, a rumour which later turned out to be false. But it gave the English vital time to muster an army and they chased Bonnie Prince Charlie and his men north until the Jacobites were decisively beaten at the Battle of Culloden in April 1746.

Bonnie Prince Charlie's narrow escape by rowing boat to Skye, aided by Flora MacDonald, who disguised him as her maid, is legendary. He returned to the continent to live out his life in exile and despite several other plans to regain the throne, he would never have another chance to rule. He died in Rome in 1788, no doubt regretting what might have been had his army not turned around at Derby.

Knit Head, Body Front, Body Back
& Arms as per Basic Doll

LEGS

COLOUR 1

Size 10/3.25mm needles
- Cast on 20
- 1st row: P
- 2nd row: K
- 3rd row: P
- 4th row: K6, K2tog, K1, K2tog, K1, K2tog, K6 (17sts)
- 5th row: P
- 6th row: K4, cast off 9, K3 (8sts)
- 7th row: P, pulling 2 sections of 4 together
- Work 4 rows SS starting with K
- 12th row: K1, inc in next, K4, inc in next, K1 (10sts)
- Work 7 rows SS starting with P
- 20th row: K1, inc in next, K6, inc in next, K1 (12sts)
- Work7 rows SS starting with P
- 28th row: K1, inc in next, K8, inc in next, K1 (14sts)
- Work 5 rows SS starting with P
- Change to Flesh colour:
- Work 10 rows SS starting with K
- Cast off

To make up: Join seam. Pull top of foot together. Stuff.

COAT

Advise working on double-ended needles to help with setting aside skirt pieces.

FRONT SKIRT SECTION – LEFT SIDE:
COLOUR 6
- Cast on 28
- 1st row: K
- 2nd row: K1, P to end, K1
- 3rd row: K

- 4th row: K1, P to end, K1
- 5th row: K
- 6th row: K1, P to end, K1
- 7th row: K1, K2tog, K2, K2tog, K2, K2tog, K2, K2tog, K11, inc in next, K1 (25sts)
- 8th row: K1, P to end, K1
- 9th row: K15, K2tog, K8 (24sts)
- 10th row: K1, P to end, K1
- 11th row: K
- 12th row: K1, P to end, K1
- 13th row: K1, K2tog, K1, K2tog, K1, K2tog, K1, K2tog, K10, inc in next, K1 (21sts)
- 14th row: K1, P to end, K1
- 15th row: K
- 16th row: K1, P to end, K1
- 17th row: K13, K2tog, K4, inc in next, K1 (21sts)
- 18th row: K1, P to end, K1
- 19th row: K1, K2tog, K2tog, K2tog, K2tog, K12 (17sts)
- 20th row: K1, P to end, K1
- 21st row: K12, K2tog, K1, inc in next, K1 (17sts)
- 22nd row: K1, P to end, K1
- 23rd row: K1, K2tog, K2tog, K12 (15sts)
- 24th row: K1, P to end, K1
- 25th row: sll, K2tog, psso, cast off 1, K9, inc in next, K1 (13sts)

Set aside on needle

BACK SKIRT SECTION – LEFT SIDE:
COLOUR 6
- Cast on 22
- 1st row: K
- 2nd row: K1, P to end, K1
- 3rd row: K
- 4th row: K1, P to end, K1
- 5th row: K1, K2tog, K19 (21sts)
- 6th row: K1, P to end, K1
- 7th row: K10, K2tog, K2, K2tog, K2,

K2tog, K1 (18sts)
- 8th row: K1, P to end, K1
- 9th row: K
- 10th row: K1, P to end, K1
- 11th row: K1, K2tog, K15 (17sts)
- 12th row: K1, P to end, K1
- 13th row: K8, K2tog, K1, K2tog, K1, K2tog, K1 (14sts)
- 14th row: K1, P to end, K1
- 15th row: K
- 16th row: K1, P to end, K1
- 17th row: K1, K2tog, K11 (13sts)
- 18th row: K1, P to end, K1
- 19th row: K6, K2tog, K2tog, K2tog, K1 (10sts)
- 20th row: K1, P to end, K1
- 21st row: K
- 22nd row: K1, P to end, K1
- 23rd row: K1, K2tog, K3, K2tog, K2tog (7sts)
- 24th row: K1, P to end, K1
- 25th row: K4, K2tog, cast off 1 (5sts)

Set aside on needle with front section left-side

BACK SKIRT SECTION – RIGHT SIDE:
COLOUR 6
- Cast on 22
- 1st row: K
- 2nd row: K1, P to end, K1
- 3rd row: K
- 4th row: K1, P to end, K1
- 5th row: K19, K2tog, K1 (21sts)
- 6th row: K1, P to end, K1
- 7th row: K1, K2tog, K2, K2tog, K2, K2tog, K10 (18sts)
- 8th row: K1, P to end, K1
- 9th row: K
- 10th row: K1, P to end, K1
- 11th row: K15, K2tog, K1 (17sts)
- 12th row: K1, P to end, K1
- 13th row: K1, K2tog, K1, K2tog, K1, K2tog, K8 (14sts)

- 14th row: K1, P to end, K1
- 15th row: K
- 16th row: K1, P to end, K1
- 17th row: K11, K2tog, K1 (13sts)
- 18th row: K1, P to end, K1
- 19th row: K1, K2tog, K2tog, K2tog, K6 (10sts)
- 20th row: K1, P to end, K1
- 21st row: K
- 22nd row: K1, P to end, K1
- 23rd row: K2tog, K2tog, K3, K2tog, K1 (7sts)
- 24th row: K1, P to end, K1
- 25th row: K2tog, cast off 1, K4 (5sts)

Set aside on needle with front & back left side

- -

FRONT SKIRT SECTION – RIGHT SIDE:
COLOUR 6
- Cast on 28
- 1st row: K
- 2nd row: K1, P to end, K1
- 3rd row: K
- 4ht row: K1, P to end, K1
- 5th row: K
- 6th row: K1, P to end, K1
- 7th row: K1, inc in next, K11, K2tog, K2, K2tog, K2, K2tog, K2, K2tog, K1 (25sts)
- 8th row: K1, P to end, K1
- 9th row: K8, K2tog, K15 (24sts)
- 10th row: K1, P to end, K1
- 11th row: K
- 12th row: K1, P to end, K1
- 13th row: K1, inc in next, K10 K2tog, K1, K2tog, K1, K2tog, K1, K2tog, K1 (21sts)
- 14th row: K1, P to end, K1
- 15th row: K
- 16th row: K1, P to end, K1
- 17th row: K1, inc in next, K4, K2tog, K13 (21sts)
- 18th row: K1, P to end, K1

- 19th row: K12, K2tog, K2tog, K2tog, K2tog, K1 (17sts)
- 20th row: K1, P to end, K1
- 21st row: K1, inc in next, K1, K2tog, K12 (17sts)
- 22nd row: K1, P to end, K1
- 23rd row: K12, K2tog, K2tog, K1 (15sts)
- 24th row: K1, P to end, K1
- 25th row: K1, inc in next, K9, K2tog, pull wool through last 2sts (13sts)

Add to needle with other skirt sections

JACKET BODY
COLOUR 6
Working 36 stitches of all skirt section: with right-side facing join wool:
Start knitting from right-side front edge
- 1st row: K
- 2nd row: K1, P to end, K1
- 3rd row: K
- 4th row: K1, P to end, K1
- 5th row: K row - inc in 2nd & 35th stitch (38sts)
- 6th row: K1, P to end, K1
- 7th row: K
- 8th row: K1, P to end, K1
- 9th row: K
- 10th row: K1, P to end, K1
- 11th row: K
- 12th row: K1, P to end, K1
- 13th row: K1, inc in next, K6, K2tog, K1, K2tog, K12, K2tog, K1, K2tog, K6, inc in next, K1 (36sts)
- 14th row: K1, P to end, K1
- 15th row: K

- -

TO CREATE LEFT FRONT:
- 16th row: K1, P9, turn –
- 17th row: K10
- 18th row: K1, P9
- 19th row: K10
- 20th row: K1, P9

- 21st row: K10
- 22nd row: K1, P2tog, P7 (9sts)
- 23rd row: K
- 24th row: K1, P2tog, P6 (8sts)
- 25th row: K
- 26th row: K1, P2tog, P2tog, P3 (6sts)
- 27the row: K, cast off 2, K3 (4sts)
- 28th row: K1, P3
- Cast off 4

- -

TO CREATE BACK:
With wrong side facing:
- 16th row: P16, turn –
- Work 12 rows SS starting with K (16sts)
- Cast off K-wise on wrong side

- -

TO CREATE RIGHT FRONT:
- 16th row: K10 with right side facing
- 17th row: P9, K1
- 18th row: K10
- 19th row: P9, K1
- 20th row: K10
- 21st row: P9, K1
- 22nd row: K1, K2tog, K7 (9sts)
- 23rd row: P8, K1
- 24th row: K1, K2tog, K6 (8sts)
- 25th row: P7, K1
- 26th row: K1, K2tog, K2tog, K3 (6sts)
- 27th row: Cast off 2, P2, K1 (4sts)
- 28th row: K
- Cast off

To make-up: Join shoulder seam.
Tidy skirt section joins. Add gold braid to edge of coat.

SLEEVES – MAKE TWO
COLOUR 6
- Cast on 28
- Work 4 rows SS starting with K
- 5th row: K10, K2tog, K4, K2tog, K10 (26sts)
- Work 3 rows SS starting with P

- 9th row: K10, K2tog, K2, K2tog, K10 (24sts)
- Work 3 rows SS starting with P
- 13th row: (K1, K2tog) to end (16sts)
- 14th row: P
- 15th row: (K2, K2tog) to end (12sts)
- Work 4 rows SS starting with P
- 20th row: K row – inc 1st & last st (14sts)
- Work 5 rows SS starting with P
- 26th row: K row – inc 1st & last st (16sts)
- Work 4 rows SS starting with P
- 31st row: P row – cast off 3, P to end (13sts)
- 32nd row: K row – cast off 3, K to end (10sts)
- 33rd row: P
- Cast off

To make up: Join sleeve seams. Turn back cuff. Add decorative lace around cuffs using crochet chains of white cotton. Inset into jacket body armholes.

BREECHES

COLOUR 4
Size 10/3.25mm needles

TO CREATE RIGHT LEG:
- Cast on 20
- 1st row: K
- 2nd row: K
- 3rd row: K
- 4th row: K2, inc in next 16 sts, K2 (36sts)
- Work 23 rows in SS starting with P
- 28th row: K2tog, cast off 3 (32sts)
- 29th row: P2tog, cast off 3 (28sts)
- 30th row: K
- 31st row: P

Set aside on needle

TO CREATE LEFT LEG:
- Work rows 1-31
- 32nd row: K27 from left leg, Ktog last st from left leg with 1st st from right leg, K27 (55sts)
- 33rd row: P
- 34th row: K
- 35th row: P7, P2tog, P6, P2tog, P21, P2tog, P6, P2tog, P7 (51sts)
- 36th row: K
- 37th row: P2tog, P23, P2tog, P22, P2tog (48sts)
- 38th row: K11, K2tog, K5, K2tog, K8, K2tog, K5, K2tog, K11 (44sts)
- 39th row: P
- 40th row: K5, K2tog, K8, K2tog, K10, K2tog, K8, K2tog, K5 (40sts)
- 41st row: P
- 42nd row: K
- 43rd row: K
- 44th row: K
- Cast off

To make up: Join seams. Add to doll.

WAISTCOAT

COLOUR 5
Size 10/3.25mm needles

LEFT SIDE
- Cast on 16
- 1st row: K
- 2nd row: K1, P to end, K1
- 3rd row: K
- 4th row: K1, P to end, K1
- 5th row: K
- 6th row: K1, P6, P2tog, P4, P2tog, K1 (14sts)
- 7th row: K12, inc in next, K1 (15sts)
- 8th row: K1, P to end, K1
- 9th row: K1, K2tog, K12 (14sts)
- 10th row: K1, P to end, K1
- 11th row: K12, inc in next, K1 (15sts)
- 12th row: K1, P11, P22tog, K1 (14sts)

- 13th row: K
- 14th row: K1, P5, P2tog, P5, K1 (13sts)
- 15th row: K1, K2tog, K8, inc in next, K1 (13sts)
- 16th row: K1, P to end, K1
- 17th row: K
- 18th row: K1, P2, P2tog, P7, K1
- 19th row: K1, K2tog, K7, inc in next, K1 (12sts)
- 20th row: K1, P to end, K1 (13sts)
- 21st row: K10, inc in next, K1
- 22nd row: K1, P to end, K1
- 23rd row: K1, K2tog, K10 (12sts)
- 24th row: K1, P to end, K1
- 25th row: K
- 26th row: K1, P to end, K1
- 27th row: K1, K2tog, K9 (11sts)
- 28th row: K1, P to end, K1
- 29th row: K
- 30th row: K1, P to end, K1
- 31st row: K
- 32nd row: K1, P7, P2tog, K1 (10sts)
- 33rd row: K
- 34th row: K1, P to end, K1
- 35th row: K1, K2tog, K7 (9sts)
- 36th row: K1, P to end, K1
- 37th row: K
- 38th row: K1, P to end, K1
- 39th row: K6, K2tog, K1 (8sts)
- 40th row: K1, P to end, K1
- 41st row: K
- 42nd row: K1, P2tog, P4, K1 (7sts)
- 43rd row: K
- 44th row: K1, P to end, K1
- 45th row: K1, K2tog, K2tog, K2tog (4sts)
- 46th row: K1, P to end, K1
- 47th row: K
- 48th row: K1, P to end, K1
- 49th row: K
- Cast off

RIGHT SIDE
- Cast on 16

- 1st row: K
- 2nd row: K1, P to end, K1
- 3rd row: K
- 4th row: K1, P to end, K1
- 5th row: K
- 6th row: K1, P2tog, P4, P2tog, P6, K1 (14sts)
- 7th row: K1, inc in next, K12 (15sts)
- 8th row: K1, P to end, K1
- 9th row: K12, K2tog, K1 (14sts)
- 10th row: K1, P to end, K1
- 11th row: K1, inc in next, K12 (15sts)
- 12th row: K1, P2tog, P11, K1 (14sts)
- 13th row: K
- 14th row: K1, P5, P2tog, P5, K1 (13sts)
- 15th row: K1, inc in next, K8, K2tog, K1 (13sts)
- 16th row: K1, P to end, K1
- 17th row: K
- 18th row: K1, P7, P2tog, P2, K1 (12sts)
- 19th row: K1, inc in next, K7, K2tog, K1 (12sts)
- 20th row: K1, P to end, K1
- 21st row: K1, inc in next, K10 (13sts)
- 22nd row: K1, P to end, K1
- 23rd row: K10, K2tog, K1 (12sts)
- 24th row: K1, P to end, K1
- 25th row: K
- 26th row: K1, P to end, K1
- 27th row: K9, K2tog, K1 (11sts)
- 28th row: K1, P to end, K1
- 29th row: K
- 30th row: K1, P to end, K1
- 31st row: K
- 32nd row: K1, P2tog, P7, K1 (10sts)
- 33rd row: K
- 34th row: K1, P to end, K1
- 35th row: K7, K2tog, K1 (9sts)
- 36th row: K1, P to end, K1
- 37th row: K
- 38th row: K1, P to end, K1
- 39th row: K1, K2tog, K6 (8sts)
- 40th row: K1, P to end, K1
- 41st row: K

- 42nd row: K1, P4, P2tog, K1 (7sts)
- 43rd row: K
- 44th row: K1, P to end, K1
- 45th row: K2tog, K2tog, K2tog, K1 (4sts)
- 46th row: K1, P to end, K1
- 47th row: K
- 48th row: K1, P to end, K1
- 49th row: K
- Cast off

To make up: Join centre front. Add beads as buttons.

SHIRT FRONT
COLOUR 3
Size 13 /2.25mm needle
- Cast on 27
- Work 7 rows SS
- Cast off

To make up: Sew around neck

STOCK/JABOT
COLOUR 3
Size 13/2.25mm needles
- Cast on 12
- Work 45 rows in SS
- Cast off

To make up: Sew into bunch and attach to neck. Add decorative lace detail by making crochet chains with white cotton.

SASH
COLOUR 7
Size 11/3mm needles
- Cast on 50 – insert a tag
- Cast on 43
- 1st row: P
- 2nd row: K1, K2tog, K45, K2tog, K40, K2tog, K1
- 3rd row: P1, P2tog, P84, P2tog, P1

- 4th row: K1, K2tog, K42, K2tog, K38, K2tog, K1
- 5th row: K1, k2tog, cast off to last 3st, K2tog, K1
- Cast off

To make up: Use mark for shoulder position. Attach to doll across body. Make tassel where sash ends join at right hip.

HAIR
Create rolled wig effect as per photo, using white fluffy wool (Colour 8) sewn in loops. With crochet hook add longer lengths to tie into pony tail.

SHOES
COLOUR 9
Size 10/3.25mm needles
- Cast on 15
- 1st row: K9, turn –
- 2nd row: P7, turn –
- 3rd row: K13
- 4th row: P15
- 5th row: sl2, K6, turn –
- 6th row: P6, turn
- 7th row: K13
- 8th row: Cast off 6, P8
- 9th row: K9
- 10th row: P5, turn –
- 11th row: K5
- 12th row: Cast on 5, P12, turn –
- 13th row: K12
- 14th row: P14
- 15th row: sl2, K6, turn –
- 16th row: P6, turn –
- 17th row: K12
- 18th row: Cast off 6, P7
- 19th row: Cast off 8

- -
FRONT TAB:
Pick-up 4 st from centre-front section with right side facing.

- 1st row: P
- 2nd row: K
- 3rd row: P
- 4th row: inc in 2nd & 3rd (6sts)
- 5th row: P
- Cast off

HEEL:
COLOUR 6
Size 11/3.00mm
Join back heel seam of shoe
   Pick-up 8 st evenly along heel edge
of shoe
- 1st row: P
- 2nd row: K1, K2tog, K2, K2tog, K1 (6sts)
- 3rd row: P1, P2tog, P2tog, P1 (4sts)
- 4th row: K2tog, K2tog (2sts)
- 5th row: P
- 6th row: K2tog, pull thread through

To make up: Join sole seam. Pull heel shape together. Wet the shoes, dab-out excess water, poke into shape. Allow to dry. Add decorative buckles made of millinery wire & fine gold twine.

TO CREATE FACE

Reference a portrait of Bonnie Prince Charlie and use wool in similar tones for eyes, eyebrows and mouth. The nose is made from a crocheted chain folded over at the end and stitched on. Rosy-up cheeks with pastel pencil.

You will need

Billy Connolly

MATERIALS:
Colour Codes:
1 Rowan Fine Tweed 100% Wool
   'Skipton' (for denim)
2 SMC Select Extra Soft Merino Black
3 SMC Select Violena White
4 Debbie Bliss Andes Silver Grey (for
   hair, beard & eyebrows)

Embroidery threads for tattoo
Stuffing

NEEDLES:
Size 10/3.25mm
Size 10/3.25mm double-ended
Crochet hook

Banana Boots

MATERIALS:
Colour Codes:
1 Sublime Cashmere Merino Silk DK
   (Yellow shade 0250)
2 Sirdar Snuggly DK (Brown shade
   0200)

Stuffing

NEEDLES:
Size 10/3.25mm

Billy Connolly
and
Banana Boots

Billy Connolly is one of the funniest men ever to come out of Scotland. Born in 1942, 'The Big Yin' worked in the Glasgow shipyards and started his entertainment career as a folk singer with the Humblebums, before gradually using his trademark sense of humour to become a hugely successful comedian. Famous for his 1970s Banana Boots and ribald humour, Billy is married to Pamela Stephenson, comedienne turned psychologist, and is known around the world both for his stand-up shows and his TV and film work, including *Mrs Brown* with Judi Dench, who was nominated for an Academy Award for her performance. Billy is a lifelong fan of Celtic Football Club and when he's in Scotland he is often seen at Celtic Park on match days. These days, however, his work takes him all round the world, most recently to New Zealand to play Dain Ironfoot, the great dwarf warrior, in Sir Peter Jackson's movie adaptation of *The Hobbit*.

Knit Head, Body Front, Body Back
& Arms as per Basic Doll

BEARD

COLOUR 4

Size 10/3.25mm needles

- Cast on 6
- 1st row: K2, cast off 2, K2 (5sts)
- 2nd row: K2, wool over twice, K2
- 3rd row: K2, K into wool over twice, K2
- 4th row: K6
- 5th row: K2tog, K2, K2tog
- 6th row: K4
- 7th row: K2tog, K2tog
- 8th row: K2tog, pull wool through

LEGS

COLOUR 2

- Cast on 20
- 1st row: P
- 2nd row: K
- 3rd row: P
- 4th row: K6, K2tog, K1, K2tog, K1, K2tog, K6 (17sts)
- 5th row: P
- 6th row: K4, cast off 9, K3 (8sts)
- 7th row: P, pulling 2 sections of 4 together
- Work 4 rows SS starting with K
- 12th row: K1, inc in next, K4, inc in next, K1 (10sts)
- Work 9 rows SS starting with P
- 22nd row: K1, inc in next, K6, inc in next, K1 (12sts)
- Work 9 rows SS starting with P
- 32nd row: K1, inc in next, K8, inc in next, K1 (14sts)
- Work 17 rows SS starting with P
- Cast off

BILLY CONNOLLY'S JEANS

COLOUR 1

Size 10

- Cast on 20
- Work 3 rows K
- Work 19 rows SS
- 23rd row: K1, inc in next, K16, inc in next, K1 (22sts)
- Work 13 rows SS starting with P
- 37th row: K row – inc in 12th (23sts)
- 38TH row: P row – cast off 2, P to end (21sts)
- 39th row: K row – cast off 2, K to end (19sts)
- 40th row: P
- Put on pin

Repeat rows 1-40 to create second leg of jeans

To knit the pair of legs together:
Starting on left-leg K18, K next st tog with 1st st of right leg, K18(37sts)

- Work 8 rows SS starting with P
- 50th row: join in black – P row
- 51st row: K in black
- 52nd row: join in denim – P row
- Cast off

To make up: Join seams. Embroider belt loops over the black belt.

BILLY CONNOLLY'S T-SHIRT

COLOUR 3

- Cast on 45 on double-ended needles
- Work 26 rows K
- Put onto 2 needles – 22 for front of shirt, 23 for back of shirt

FRONT:
- Work 4 rows SS starting with P

- 5th row: P row – cast off 5, P to end
- 6th row: K row – cast off 5, K to end
- 7th row: P
- Cast off

BACK:
- Work 4 rows SS starting with K
- 5th row: K row – cast off 5, K to end
- 6th row: P row – cast off 5, P to end
- Cast off

To make up: Join shoulder seams.
-

HAIR

COLOUR 4

- Cast on 40
- Work 9cm in SS
- Cast off

To make up: Steam-press knitting. Unpick to create crinkly wool. Cut into approx 5-inch lengths and knot onto head using a crochet hook.

TO CREATE FACE

Billy Connolly has a gift of a face with many different expressions. Working from an image use yarn of a similar tone for the eyes. Eyebrows and beard are worked in the same yarn as the hair. The nose is a substantial crocheted chain. As you work, think 'funny'!

Banana Boots

RIGHT BOOT
COLOUR 1

RIGHT SIDE
- Cast on 5
- 1st row: K
- 2nd row: P
- 3rd row: K
- 4th row: P
- 5th row: K2, inc in next, K1, inc in next (7sts)
- 6th row: P
- 7th row: K4, inc in next, K1, inc in next (9sts)
- 8th row: P5, turn –
- 9th row: K5
- 10th row: P9
- 11th row: K9
- 12th row: P5, turn –
- 13th row: K5
- 14th row: P9
- 15th row: K9
- 16th row: P5, turn –
- 17th row: K5
- 18th row: P9
- 19th row: K9
- 20th row: P5, turn –
- 21st row: K5
- 22nd row: P9
- 23rd row: K9
- 24th row: P5, turn –
- 25th row: K4, inc in last (6sts)
- 26th row: P10
- 27th row: K10
- 28th row: P6, turn –
- 29th row: K6
- 30th row: P10
- 31st row: K10
- 32nd row: P6, turn –
- 33rd row: K6
- 34th row: P10

- 35th row: K10
- 36th row: P10
- For front tab on right side:
- 1st row: K2, inc in next, K2, turn –
- 2nd row: P
- 3rd row: K
- 4th row: P
- 5th row: K4, K2tog (5sts)
- 6th row: P
- 7th row: K3, K2tog (4sts)
- 8th row: P
- 9th row: K2 tog, K2tog (2sts)

TO CREATE STEM:
Join in brown wool
- Work 2 rows of 2st i-cord
- Inc in 1st (3sts)
- Work 4 rows of 3st i-cord
- Cast off 3

TO CREATE BACK TAB:
Use remaining 5 sts:
With right side facing, work rows 1-9
Pull wool through

RIGHT BOOT – LEFT SIDE
- Cast on 5
- 1st row: K
- 2nd row: P
- 3rd row: K
- 4th row: P
- 5th row: inc in 1st & 3rd, K to end (7sts)
- 6th row: P7
- 7th row: K row – inc 1st & 3rd, K to end (9sts)
- 8th row: P9
- 9th row: K5, turn –
- 10th row: P5
- 11th row: K9
- 12th row: P9
- 13th row: K5, turn –
- 14th row: P5

- 15th row: K9
- 16th row: P9
- 17th row: K5, turn –
- 18th row: P5
- 19th row: K9
- 20th row: P9
- 21st row: K5, turn –
- 22nd row: P5
- 23rd row: K9
- 24th row: P9
- 25th row: K row – inc in 1st, K4, turn –
- 26th row: P6
- 27th row: K10
- 28th row: P9
- 29th row: K6, turn –
- 30th row: P6
- 31st row: K10
- 32nd row: P10
- 33rd row: K6, turn –
- 34th row: P6
- 35th row: K10
- 36th row: P10

TO CREATE BACK TAB:
1st row: K2, inc in next, K2, turn –
- 2nd row: P
- 3rd row: K
- 4th row: P
- 5th row: K2tog, K4 (5sts)
- 6th row: P
- 7th row: K2tog, K3 (4sts)
- 8th row: P
- 9th row: K2tog, K2tog (2sts)

Pull wool through

TO CREATE FRONT TAB:
Work in remaining 5sts:
Work rows 1-9
Pull wool through

LEFT BOOT

COLOUR I

RIGHT SIDE
Work as for right boot right side from
rows 1-36
Work both tab rows 1-9
Finish both by pulling wool through

LEFT SIDE
Work as for right boot left side from
rows 1-36
Work back tab rows 1-9
Work front tab rows 1-9
Use final 2sts to create stem as before

HEEL – MAKE TWO

COLOUR 2
- Cast on 9
- 1st row: K
- 2nd row: P
- 3rd row: K2tog at each end (7sts)
- 4th row: P
- 5th row: K2tog at each end (5sts)
- 6th row: P
- 7th row: K2tog at each end (3sts)
- Cast off

To make up:
Sew front seams together to base of tabs.
Sew underfoot/back seam together to
base of tabs, leaving gap for heel. Fold
heel piece vertically. Sew cast on edge
of heel together. Sew sides of heel into
boot.

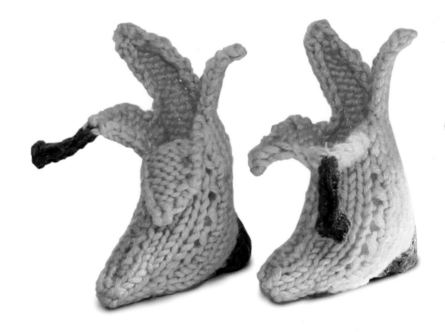

Andy Murray

Andy Murray is the most successful Scottish tennis player of all time and is a national hero. His 2012 gold medal victory at the London Olympics was followed soon after by his first major win at the US Open in New York, the first major singles win by a British male tennis player since Fred Perry in 1936. The match was a five-set thriller and kept a bleary-eyed nation up to the wee small hours as Murray and Novak Djokovic traded blows until Andy finally won.

Born in Dunblane in 1987, Andy was a talented sportsman and could have tried his luck at football instead of tennis. But with the backing of his tennis champion mother Judy, Andy obviously made the right choice and is now one of the world's best players. In an era which boasts Roger Federer, Rafa Nadal and Novak Djokovic, winning his first Grand Slam was not easy, but with new coach and eight-time Grand Slam winner Ivan Lendl on his team, Andy Murray now looks set for further success.

Knit Body Front, Body Back & Arms as per Basic Doll

LEGS – MAKE TWO

COLOUR 2

Size 10/3.25mm needles
- Cast on 20
- 1st row: P
- 2nd row: K
- 3rd row: P
- 4th row: K6, K2tog, K1, K2tog, K1, K2tog, K6 (17sts)
- 5th row: P
- 6th row: K4, cast off 9, K3 (8sts)
- 7th row: K to end, pulling 2 sets of 4st tog
- 8th row: work in 1in1 rib
- 9th row: work in 1in1 rib
- 10th row: work in 1in1rib – inc in 1st & last (10sts)
- 11th row: rib
- 12th row: rib
- 13th row: K
- Join Colour 1:
- Work 6 rows SS starting with K row
- 20th row: K row – inc 1st & last (12sts)
- Work 9 rows SS starting with P row
- 30th row: K row – inc 1st & last (14sts)
- Work 17 rows SS starting with P row
- Cast off

To make up:
Join side seam. Pull top of shoe together & add lace (strand of knitting cotton). Embroider stripes on shoes.

HEAD – MAKE TWO PIECES

COLOUR 1

Size 10/3.25mm needles
- Cast on 6
- 1st row: K
- 2nd row: P
- 3rd row: K row – inc in 1st & last (8sts)
- 4th row: P
- 5th row: K row – inc in 1st & last (10sts)
- 6th row: P
- 7th row: K row – inc in 1st & last (12sts)
- 8th row: P
- 9th row: K row – inc in 1st & last (14sts)
- Work 9 rows SS starting with P
- 19th row: K1, sl1, K1, psso, K8, K2tog, K1 (12sts)
- 20th row: P
- 21st row: K1, sl1, K1, psso, K6, K2tog, K1 (10sts)
- 22nd row: P
- Cast off

To make up: Join two pieces. Stuff. Sew to body.

SHORTS

COLOUR 3

Size 10/3.25mm needles
For right leg:
- Cast on 24
- 1st row: K
- Work 14 rows SS starting with K row
- 16th row: K row – inc in 13th (25sts)
- 17th row: cast off 2, P to end
- 18th row: cast off 2, K to end
- 19th row: P2tog, P17, P2tog (19sts)
- Put on pin
- Repeat this pattern for left leg
- 20th row: with right side facing K18, K last st of left leg tog with 1st st of right leg, K18 (37sts)
- Work 11 rows SS starting with P

- Cast off

To make up: Join inside leg seams. Attach to body.

T-SHIRT

COLOUR 3

Cast on 44 on double-ended needles
- Join to circle
- 1st row: K
- 2nd row: P
- Work 22 rows K
- Work on 2 needles:
- 25th row: turn, cast on 5, P27 (27sts)
- 26th row: turn, cast on 5, K32 (32sts)
- From here K 1st & last st of P rows
- Work 7 rows SS starting with P row
- 34th row: K row – inc in 8th & 24th (34sts)
- 35th row: P
- 36th row: K row – inc in 9th & 25th (36sts)
- 37th row: P
- Cast off
- Work on remaining 22sts on 2 needles:
- 25th row: cast on 5, P27
- 26th row: cast on 5, K32
- From here K 1st & last st of P rows
- Work 7 rows SS starting with P row
- 34th row: K row – K7, inc in next, K7, cast off 2, K6, inc in next, K7 (32sts)
- 35th row: K1, P12, P2tog, K1– turn (15sts)

- -
TO CREATE RIGHT-SIDE FRONT:
- 36th row: K1, K2tog, K3, inc in next, K to end (15sts)
- 37th row: P
- Cast off

TO CREATE LEFT-SIDE FRONT:
- Rejoin wool to remaining 16sts wrong side facing:
- 35th row: K1, P2tog, P12, K1 (15sts)
- 36th row: K row - inc in 9th, K3, K2tog, K1
- 37th row: P
- Cast off

To make up: Join shoulder seams. Join underarm seams. Embroider stripes

ARMBANDS – MAKE TWO
COLOUR 2
- Size 13/2.25mm needles
- Cast on 4
- Work 10 rows GS
- Join in blue – work 8 rows SS
- Join in white – work 10 rows GS
- Cast off

To make up: Embroider Saltire Cross in white on blue section. Sew around wrist.

HAIR
COLOUR 4
Size 10/3.25mm needles
- Cast on 5
- Work 2 rows GS
- 3rd row: K2, inc in next, K2 (6sts)
- 4th row: inc in 3rd & 4th st (8sts)
- 5th row: K2, inc in next, K2, inc in next, K2 (10sts)
- 6th row: K
- 7th row: K2, inc in next, K4, inc in next, K2 (12sts)
- Work 3 rows
- 11th row: cast on 5, K to end (17sts)
- 12th row: cast on 5, K to end (22sts)
- 13th row: K
- 14th row: K2tog, K4, inc in next, K8, inc in next, K4, K2tog (22sts)
- 15th row: K
- 16th row: K2tog, K4, inc in next, K8, inc in next, K4, K2tog (22sts)
- Work 3 rows
- 20th row: K2, K2tog, K1, K2tog, K3, K2tog, K3, K2tog, K1, K2tog, K2 (17sts)
- 21st row: K
- 22nd row: K3, K2tog, K1, K2tog, K1, K2tog, K1, K2tog, K3 (12sts)
- 23rd row: K2tog, K1, K2tog, K2, K2tog, K1, K2tog (8sts)
- Work 2 rows
- 26th row: K2tog, K4, K2tog (6sts)
- 27th row: K
- 28th row: K2tog, K2, K2tog (4sts)
- 29th row: K
- 30th row: K2tog, K2tog (2sts)
- Pull wool through

To make up: Sew to head as per photo.

TO CREATE FACE

Working from a photo is useful. Choose a typical expression, and using own choice of wool stitch on eyes, eyebrows and mouth. The nose and ears are crocheted chains in flesh colour, stitched on.

TENNIS RACQUET

Cut a length of boning and loop into racquet shape. Place dowel between the ends to form a handle. Glue in place. Wrap handle in blue wool. Take length of twine and with needle pierce through boning to create racquet strings. Paint frame in black & red.

What a winner!

You will need

MATERIALS:
(1 × 50g ball of each colour unless otherwise stated)
Colour Codes:
1 Gedifra Riana Green
(shade 03469) – 2× 50g balls
2 Rowan Cotton Glaze Green
(shade 812) – 2× 50g balls
3 Sublime Lustrous Extra-fine Merino
DK (Yellow shade 293)
4 Debbie Bliss Prima pale (Green
shade 35733)
5 Sublime Lustrous Extra-fine
Merino DK (Green shade 335)
6 Rowan Fine Tweed
(Brown shade 373)
7 Rowan Fine Lace
(Red shade 00935)
8 Rowan Fine Lace
(Gold shade 00930)

Beads/buttons (for eyes)
Feathers/Brooch (for hat)
False eyelashes
Stuffing

NEEDLES:
Size 10/3.25mm
Size 10/3.25mm double-ended
Size 12/2.75mm

Nessie

The Loch Ness Monster remains a creature of mystery and legend. Many have tried to find Nessie, some even claim to have photographs, but the definitive proof remains elusive. Modern Nessie-spotting began with a sighting in 1933 and Hugh Gray's photograph of that year led to feverish speculation about the Monster. Since then there have been many expeditions to find the Loch Ness Monster and a number of reported sightings, but the search still goes on. As yet, we don't even know if Nessie is a boy or a girl, or maybe there are both, so ours is Miss Nessie, with an added touch of glamour. And, as Loch Ness is the largest, deepest freshwater loch in the Highlands with its deepest parts at 230m (or 750ft), Nessie, or Miss Nessie, has plenty of places to hide from prying eyes.

BODY

COLOUR 1 & 2 KNITTED TOGETHER FOR BOTH LEFT AND RIGHT SIDES

LEFT SIDE
- Cast on 2
- Work 3 rows SS starting with P
- 4th row: K row – inc in every stitch   (4sts)
- Work 11 rows SS starting with P
- 16th row: K2, inc in next, K1   (5sts)
- Work 7 SS starting with P
- 24th row: K2, inc in next, K2   (6sts)
- Work 5 rows SS starting with P
- 30th row: K4, turn –
- 31st row: P4
- 32nd row: K6
- 33rd row: P
- 34th row: K1, inc in next, K2, inc in next, K1   (8sts)
- 35th row: P
- 36th row: K5, turn –
- 37th row: P5
- Work 4 rows SS starting with K
- 42nd row: K3, inc in next, K4   (9sts)
- Work 3 rows SS starting with P
- 46th row: K2, inc in next, K3, inc in next, K2   (11sts)
- Work 8 rows SS starting with P
- 55th row: P7, turn –
- 56th row: K7
- 57th row: P11
- 58th row: K5, inc in next, K5   (12sts)
- 59th row: P8, turn –
- 60th row: K8
- 61st row: P6, turn –
- 62nd row: K6
- 63rd row: P
- 64th row: K
- 65th row: P7, turn –
- 66th row: K7
- 67th row: P
- 68th row: K3, inc in next, K4, inc in next, K3   (14sts)
- 69th row: P10, turn –
- 70th row: K10
- 71st row: P8, turn –
- 72nd row: K8

RIGHT SIDE
- Cast on 2
- Work 2 rows SS starting with K
- 3rd row: inc in both sts   (4sts)
- Work 13 rows SS starting with P
- 17th row: K2, inc in next, K1 (5sts)
- Work 7 SS starting with P
- 25th row: K2, inc in next, K2 (6sts)
- Work 4 rows SS starting with P
- 30th row: P4, turn –
- 31st row: K4
- 32nd row: P6
- 33rd row: K
- 34th row: P
- 35th row: K1, inc in next, K2, inc in next, K1(8sts)
- 36th row: P5, turn –
- 37th row: K5
- Work 5 rows SS starting with P
- 43rd row: K4, inc in next, K3 (9sts)
- Work 3 rows SS starting with P
- 47th row: K2, inc in next, K3, inc in next, K2   (11sts)
- Work 7 rows SS starting with P
- 55th row: K7, turn –
- 56th row: P7
- 57th row: K11
- 58th row: P11
- 59th row: K1, inc in next, K5, turn –
- 60th row: P8
- 61st row: K6, turn –
- 62nd row: P6
- 63rd row: K12
- 64th row: P12
- 65th row: K7, turn –
- 66th row: P7
- 67th row: K
- 68th row: P
- 69th row: K1, inc in next, K3, inc in next, K2, turn –
- 70th row: P10
- 71st row: K8, turn –
- 72nd row: P8

- 73rd row: P
- 74th row: K7, inc in next, K6   (15sts)
- 75th row: P9, turn –
- 76th row: K9
- Work 4 rows SS starting with P
- 81st row: P9, turn –
- 82nd row: K9
- 83rd row: P
- 84th row: K5, inc in next, K3, inc in next, K5   (17sts)
- 85th row: P9, turn –
- 86th row: K9
- 87th row: P
- 88th row: K
- 89th row: P8, turn –
- 90th row: K8
- 91st row: P6, turn –
- 92ndrow. K6
- Work 4 rows SS starting with P
- 97th row: P12, turn –
- 98th row: K12
- 99th row: P9, turn –
- 100th row: K9
- 101st row: P14, turn –
- 102nd row: K14
- 103rd row: P12, turn –
- 104th row: K12
- Work 21 rows SS starting with P
- 126th row: K14, turn –
- 127th row: P14
- 128th row: K12, turn –
- 129th row: P12
- 130th row: K5, inc in next, K5, inc in next, K5   (19sts)
- 131st row: P
- 132nd row: K5, inc in next, K6, turn –
- 133rd row: P13
- 134th row: K10, turn –
- 135th row: P10
- 136th row: K20
- 137th row: P
- 138th row: K17, turn –
- 139th row: P17
- 140th row: K18, K2tog   (19sts)
- 141st row: P
- 142nd row: K7, inc in next, K7, turn –

- 73rd row: K6, inc in next, K7   (15sts)
- 74th row: P
- 75th row: K9, turn –
- 76th row: P9
- Work 4 rows SS starting with K
- 81st row: K9, turn –
- 82nd row: P9
- 83rd row: K5, inc in next, K3, inc in next, K5   (17sts)
- 84th row: P17
- 85th row: K9, turn –
- 86th row: P9
- 87th row: K17
- 88th row: P17
- 89th row: K8, turn –
- 90th row: P8
- 91st row: K6, turn –
- 92nd row: P6
- Work 4 rows SS starting with K
- 97th row: K12, turn –
- 98th row: P12
- 99th row: K9, turn –
- 100th row: P9
- 101st row: K14, turn –
- 102nd row: P14
- 103rd row: K12, turn –
- 104th row: P12
- Work 21 rows SS starting with K
- 126th row: P14, turn –
- 127th row: K14
- 128th row: P12, turn –
- 129th row: K6, inc in next, K5
- 130th row: P18
- 131st row: K10, inc in next, K7   (19sts)
- 132nd row: P12, turn –
- 133rd row: K6, inc in next, K5
- 134th row: P10, turn –
- 135th row: K10
- 136th row: P20
- 137th row: K20
- 138th row: P17, turn –
- 139th row: K17
- 140th row: P18, P2tog(19sts)
- 141st row: K19
- 142nd row: P15, turn

- Needle 2 K11 (top of head)
- Needle 3 K10 (side of face)
- Tip – to keep the circle complete catch work together under the chin i.e. the work on needle 1 & 3
- 32nd row: K2, inc in next, K5, K2tog, K11, K2tog, K5, inc in next, K2 (31sts)
- 33rd row: K
- 34th row: K2, inc in next, K10, inc in next, K3, inc in next, K10, inc in next, K2 (35sts)
- 35th row: K
- 36th row: K5, inc in next, K10, inc in next, K1, inc in next, K10, inc in next, K5 (39sts)
- Work 6 rows K
- 43rd row: K3, K2tog, K4, K2tog, K4, K2tog, K5, K2tog, K4, K2tog, K4, K2tog, K2 (32sts)
- 44th row: Ktog the final st of needle 3 with 1st st from needle 1, K to end of row
- 45th row: K1, K2tog, (K2, K2tog) to last st, K1 (24sts)
- 46th row: (K1, K2tog) to end (16sts)
- 47th row: K
- 48th row: (K2, K2tog) x 4 (12sts)
- 49th row: (K2tog) to end (6sts)

Pull wool through 6 sts – pull tight & finish off

TUMMY

COLOUR 3

Cast on 2

- Work 4 rows ss starting with K
- 5th row: inc in 1st, K1   (3sts)
- Work 3 rows ss starting with P
- 9th row: inc in middle st   (4sts)
- Work 3 rows in ss starting with P
- 13th row: K row – Join Colour 4 – K1, inc in next, K2 (5sts)

- 14th row: K
- 15th row: Join Colour 3 – K to end
- 16th row: P
- 17th row: inc in middle st (6sts)
- Work 4 rows ss starting with P
- 22nd row: Join Colour 4 – P to end
- 23rd row: P
- 24th row: Join Colour 3 – P to end
- 25th row: K2, inc in next, K3 (7sts)
- Work 3 rows SS starting with P
- 29th row: K row – inc in middle st (8sts)
- 30th row: P
- 31st row: Join Colour 4 – K to end
- 32nd row: K row
- 33rd row: Join Colour 3 – K3, inc in next, K4 (9sts)
- Work 5 rows SS starting with P
- 39th row: K row – inc in middle st (10sts)
- 40th row: Join Colour 4 – P to end
- 41st row: P
- 42nd row: Join Colour 3 – P to end
- 43rd row: K
- 44th row: P
- 45th row: K4, inc in next, K5 (11sts)
- Work 4 rows SS starting with P
- 50th row: Join Colour 4 – P to end
- 51st row: P
- 52nd row: Join Colour 3 – P to end
- 53rd row: K row – inc in middle st
- Work 5 rows SS starting with P
- 59th row: K5, inc in next, K6 (13sts)
- 60th row: Join Colour 4 – P to end
- 61st row: P
- 62nd row: K
- 63rd row: Join Colour 3 – K to end
- Work 3 rows SS starting with P
- 67th row: K row – inc in middle st (14ts)
- Work 3 rows SS starting with P
- 71st row: Join Colour 4 – K to end
- 72nd row: K
- 73rd row: P

- 74th row: Join Colour 3 – P to end
- 75th row: K6, inc in next, K7 (15sts)
- Work 7 rows SS starting with P
- 83rd row: Join Colour 4 – K to end
- 84th row: K
- 85th row: P
- 86th row: Join Colour 3 – P to end
- 87th row: K row – inc in middle st
- Work 9 rows SS starting with P
- 97th row: Join Colour 4 – K to end
- 98th row: K
- 99th row: P
- 100th row: K
- 101st row: Join Colour 3 – K to end
- Work 10 rows SS starting with P
- 112th row: Join Colour 4 – P to end
- 113th row: P
- 114th row: K
- 115th row: P
- 116th row: Join Colour 3 – P to end
- Work 10 rows SS starting with K
- 127th row: Join Colour 4 – K to end
- 128th row: K
- 129th row: P
- 130th row: K
- 131st row: Join Colour 3 – K to end
- Work 7 rows SS starting with P
- 139th row: K7, K2tog, K7 (15sts)
- 140th row: P
- 141st row: K
- 142nd row: Join Colour 4 – P to end
- 143rd row: P
- 144th row: K
- 145th row: P
- 146th row: Join Colour 3 – P to end
- Work 8 rows SS starting with K
- 155th row: Join Colour 4 – K to end
- 156th row: K
- 157th row: P
- 158th row: Join Colour 3 – P to end
- 159th row: K7, K2tog, K6 (14sts)
- Work 6 rows SS starting with P
- 166th row: P6, P2tog, P6 (13sts)
- 167th row: Join Colour 4 – K to end

- 168th row: K
- 169th row: P
- 170th row: Join Colour 3 – P to end
- Work 2 rows SS starting with K
- 173rd row: K6, K2tog, K5 (12sts)
- Work 5 rows SS starting with P
- 179th row: Join Colour 4 – K to end
- 180th row: K
- 181st row: P
- 182nd row: Join Colour 3 – P to end
- 183rd row: K5, k2tog, K5 (11sts)
- Work 7 rows SS starting with P
- 191st row: Join Colour 4 – K to end
- 192nd row: K
- 193rd row: P
- 194th row: Join Colour 3 – P to end
- 195th row: K4, K2tog, K5 (10sts)
- Work 7 rows SS starting with P
- 203rd row: Join Colour 4 – K to end
- 204th row: K
- 205th row: Join Colour 3 – K to end
- 206th row: P
- 207th row: K4, K2tog, K4 (9sts)
- Work 6 rows SS starting with P
- 214th row: Join Colour 4 – P to end
- 215th row: P
- 216th row: Join Colour 3 – P to end
- Work 4 rows SS starting with K
- 221st row: K3, K2tog, K4 (8sts)
- Work 3 rows SS starting with P
- 225th row: Join Colour 4 – K to end
- 226th row: K
- 227th row: Join Colour 3 – K to end
- 228th row: P
- 229th row: K3, K2tog, K3 (7sts)
- Work 5 rows SS starting with P
- 235th row: K3, K2tog, K2 (6sts)
- 236th row: Join Colour 4 – P to end
- 237th row: P
- 238th row: Join Colour 3 – P to end
- Work 3 rows SS starting with K
- 242nd row: P2, P2tog, P2 (5sts)
- Work 3 rows SS starting with K
- 246th row: Join Colour 4 – P to end

- 247th row: P
- 248th row: Join Colour 3 – P to end
- 249th row: K
- 250th row: P2, P2tog, P1 (4sts)
- Work 6 rows SS starting with K
- 257th row: K1, K2tog, K1 (3 sts)
- Work 4 rows SS starting with P
- 262nd row: P2tog, P1
- Work 2 rows SS starting with K

Pull wool through

FINS

COLOUR 5
Size 12/2.75mm

NECK FINS

TOP:
- Cast on 2
- 1st row: K
- 2nd row: P
- 3rd row: inc in both st (4sts)
- 4th row: P
- 5th row: K
- Work in SS with 1xK st at beginning and end of each P row, unless otherwise stated.
- 6th row: P
- 7th row: K1, inc in next 2sts, K1 (6sts)
- Work 7 rows SS starting with P
- 15th row: K1, inc in next, K2, inc in next, K1 (8sts)
- Work 3 rows SS starting with P
- 18th row: K4, turn –
- 19th row: P3, K1
- 20th row: K5, turn –
- 21st row: P4, K1
- 22nd row: K
- 23rd row: P
- Cast off

MIDDLE:
- Cast on 2
- Work rows 1-12 Top Fin
- 13th row: K4, inc in next, K1 (7sts)
- 14th row: P
- 15th row: K5, inc in next, K1 (8sts)
- 16th row: P
- 17th row: K6, inc in next, K1 (9sts)
- 18th row: P
- 19th row: K7, inc in next, K1 (10sts)
- 20th row: P
- 21st row: K8, inc in next, K1 (11sts)
- 22nd row: K1, P6, turn –
- 23rd row: K5, inc in next, K1
- 24th row: P
- Cast off

BOTTOM:
- Cast on 2
- Work rows 1-16 as Top Fin
- 17th row: K1, inc in next, K3, turn –
- 18th row: P5, K1
- 19th row: K5, turn –
- 20th row: P4, K1
- 21st row: K4, turn –
- 22nd row: P3, K1
- 23rd row: K1, inc in next, K7 (10sts)
- 24th row: P
- 25th row: K4, inc in next, K5 (11sts)
- 26th row: P
- 27th row: K4, turn –
- 28th row: P3, K1
- 29th row: K
- Cast off

MIDDLE BODY FINS
No 1 (from the front):
- Cast on 2
- Work rows 1-12 as Top Neck Fin

- 13th row: K3, turn –
- 14th row: P2, KI
- Work 4 row SS starting with K
- 19th row: K2, inc in next 2 stitches, K2
- Work 3 rows SS starting with P
- 23rd row: K5, turn –
- 24th row: P4, KI
- Work 4 rows SS starting with K
- 29th row: K6, K2tog   (7sts)
- 30th row: P
- 31st row: K4, turn –
- 32nd row: P3, KI
- 33rd row: K5, K2tog (6sts)
- Work 3 rows SS starting with P
- 37th row: K4, K2tog (5sts)
- Work 3 rows SS starting with P
- 41st row: K3, K2 tog (4sts)
- Work 3 rows SS starting with P
- 45th row: K2, K2tog (3sts)
- Work 3 rows SS starting with P
- 49th row: KI, K2tog (2sts)
- Pull wool through

NO 2:
- Cast on 2
- Work rows 1-11 as Top Neck Fin
- 12th row: K, P2, turn –
- 13th row: K3
- 14th row: P
- 15th row: K4, inc in next, KI(7sts)
- 16th row: P
- 17th row: K2, inc in next, KI, inc in next, K2 (9sts)
- Work 3 rows SS starting P
- 21st row: K2, inc in next, K3, inc in next, K2 (11sts)
- Work 7 rows SS starting P
- 29th row: K2tog, K to end (10sts)
- 30th row: P
- 31st row: K2tog, K to end (9sts)
- 32nd row: P
- 33rd row: K2tog, K2tog, K3, K2tog (6sts)
- 43rd row: P

- 35th row: K2tog, K4 (5sts)
- Work 3 rows SS starting P
- 39th row: K2tog, K3 (4sts)
- Work 3 rows SS starting P
- 43rd row: K2tog, K2tog (2sts)
- Pull wool through

NO 3:
- Cast on 2
- Work rows 1-8 as Top Neck Fin
- 9th row: KI, inc in next, K2, inc in next, KI (8sts)
- 10th row: P
- 11th row: K5, turn –
- 12th row: P4, KI
- 13th row: KI, inc in next, K4, inc in next, KI (10sts)
- 14th row: P
- 15th row: K5, turn –
- 16th row: P4, KI
- 17th row: K6, turn –
- 18th row: P5, KI
- 19th row: K7, turn –
- 20th row: P6, KI
- 21st row: K
- 22nd row: P
- 23rd row: K2, K2tog, K6 (9sts)
- 24th row: P
- 25th row: K
- 26th row: Cast off 2, P to end (7sts)
- 27th row: K2tog, K3, K2tog (5sts)
- 28th row: P
- 29th row: K3, K2tog (4sts)
- Work 4 rows SS starting P
- 34th row: P2tog, P2tog (2sts)
- Pull wool through

NO 4:
- Cast on 2
- Work rows 1 – 8 as Top Neck Fin
- 9th row: KI, inc in next, K2, inc in next, KI (8sts)
- Work 4 rows SS starting P

- 14th row: KI, P4, turn –
- 15th row: K5
- 16th row: KI, P5, turn –
- 17th row K6
- 18th row: KI, P3, turn –
- 19th row: K4
- 20th row: KI, P2, turn –
- 21st row: K3
- 22 row: P
- 23rd row: Cast off 2, K to end (6sts)
- 24th row: P
- Cast off remaining st

TAIL FINS

FRONT:

Cast on 2
- Work rows 1-10 as Neck Fin Top
- 11th row: KI, inc in next, K2, inc in next, KI (8sts)
- Work 3 rows SS starting with P
- 15th row: K4, turn –
- 16th row: P3, KI
- 17th row: K
- 18th row: P
- 19th row: K4, turn –
- 20th row: P3, KI
- 21st row: K
- 22nd row: P
- 23rd row: K5, turn –
- 24th row: P4, KI
- 25th row: K
- 26th row: P
- 27th row: K4, turn –
- 28th row: P3, KI
- 29th row: K3, turn –
- 30th row: P2, KI
- 31st row: K6, turn –
- 32nd row: P5, KI
- 33rd row: K6, turn –
- 34th row: P5, KI
- 35th row: K5, turn –
- 36th row: P4, KI
- 37th row: KI, inc in next, K2, turn –
- 38th row: P4, KI

- 39th row: K4, turn –
- 40th row: P3, K1
- 41st row: K7, make 2sts in the gap, K1 (11sts)
- 42nd row: K2tog, P8, K1 (10sts)
- Cast off

MIDDLE:
- Cast on 2
- Work rows 1-13 as Top Neck Fin
- 14th row: K1, P2, turn –
- 15th row: K3
- 16th row: P
- 17th row: K
- 18th row: K1, P3, turn –
- 19th row: K2, inc in next, K1
- 20th row: P (7sts)
- 21st row: K5, inc in next, K1 (8sts)
- 22nd row: P
- 23rd row: K1, K2tog, K5 (7sts)
- Work 3 rows SS starting with P
- 27th row: K1, K2tog, K4 (6sts)
- Work 3 rows SS starting with P
- 31st row: K1, K2tog, K3 (5sts)
- Work 3 rows SS starting with P
- 35th row: K1, K2tog, K2 (4sts)
- 36th row: P2tog, P2tog
- Pull wool through

REAR:
- Cast on 2
- Work rows 1-10 as Top Neck Fin
- 11th row: K1, inc in next, K2, inc in next, K1 (8sts)
- Work 3 rows SS starting with P
- 15th row: K5, K2tog, K1 (7sts)
- Work 3 rows SS starting with P
- 19th row: K4, K2tog, K1 (6sts)
- Work 3 rows SS starting with P
- 23rd row: K3, K2tog, K1 (5sts)
- Work 3 rows SS starting with P
- 27th row: K2, K2tog, K1 (4sts)
- 28th row: P2tog, P2tog
- Pull wool through

HAT – 3X COLOUR STRIPES

Size 10/3.25mm regular & double-ended
COLOUR 7
- Cast on 42 on regular size 10/3.25mm
- Work 3 rows SS starting with K
- 4th row: K
- Work 3 rows SS starting with K
- Put on 3 needles:
- 8th row: inc in 1st & 2nd st, (K1, inc) to end (64sts)
- 9th row: Join Colour 6
- 10th row: K
- 11th row: Join Colour 7 – K
- 12th row: K
- 13th row: Join Colour 6 – K
- 14th row: K
- 15th row: Join Colour 8 – K
- 16th row: Join Colour 6 – (inc, K1) to end (96sts)
- 17th row: K
- 18th row: K
- 19th row: Join Colour 7 – K
- 20th row: K
- 21st row: Join Colour 6 – K
- 22nd row: (K1, K2tog) to end (64sts)
- 23rd row: Join Colour 8 – K
- 24th row: Join Colour 6 – K
- 25th row: K
- 26th row: K
- 27th row: Join Colour 7 – K
- 28th row: K
- 29th row: Join Colour 6 – K
- 30th row: (K2tog) to end (32sts)
- 31st row: Join Colour 8 – K
- 32nd row: Join Colour 6 – K
- 33rd row: K
- 34th row: K
- 35th row: Join Colour 7 – (K2tog) to end (16sts)
- 36th row: K
- 37th row: Join Colour 6 – K
- 38th row: (K2tog) to end (8sts)
- 39th row: (K2tog) to end (4sts)
- Pull wool through

Embroider radiating lines in red and gold to give a tartan effect.
Make a cap badge from a brooch and feathers of your choice

To make up:
Stitch the tummy section to the side panel and finish under the chin.
Sew the centre back seam together a short way down the neck from the head and a short way along from the end of the tail.
  Stuff firmly, paying particular attention to the neck.
Press all the fin pieces carefully and then lay them out overlapping slightly till you have good overall shapes to fit along the centre back seam, catch together with a few stitches. Position and stitch them in place, close the seam completely.
Make up feather and jewelled hat badge, attach to the hat and sew at a jaunty angle onto the head.
  Add eyes and false eyelashes for that 'catch me if you can' look.

MATERIALS:
Colour Codes:
1 Stylecraft Eskimo DK Black

Black beads for eyes & nose
Tartan ribbon
Stuffing

NEEDLES:
Size 9/3.75mm (used for main
body of dog)
Size 10/3.25mm (used for ears only)

Scottish Terrier

The Scottish Terrier, or Scottie, is one of Scotland's most iconic canine friends, alongside the West Highland Terrier, or Westie, as it's perhaps better known. Originally bred to hunt rats, mice, badgers and foxes in the Scottish Highlands, nowadays Scotties are well known as lovable but occasionally feisty pets.

Famous owners have included Queen Victoria, Rudyard Kipling, Jackie Onassis and American Presidents Franklin D. Roosevelt, Dwight D. Eisenhower and George W. Bush, and Roosevelt's much-loved Scottie, Fala, now sits with him on his memorial in Washington DC.

Knitted throughout in GS

FRONT LEG – LEFT SIDE

- Cast oCast on 9
- K 2 rows
- 3rd row: K3, cast off 3, K2 (6sts)
- 4th row: K pulling 2 sets of 3 sts tog
- K 3 rows
- 8th row: inc in 1st, K1, inc in next 2sts, K1, inc in last st (10sts)
- K 3 rows
- 12th row: K5, cast off 5, put on pin for later

BACK LEG – LEFT SIDE

- Cast on 9
- K 2 rows
- 3rd row: K2, K2tog, cast off 1, K2 tog, K2 (6sts)
- K 4 rows
- 8th row: inc in 1st, K1, inc in next 2sts, K1, inc in last (10sts)
- 9th row: K
- 10th row: inc in 1st, K2, inc in next, K2, inc in next, K2, inc in last (14sts)
- K 3 rows
- 14th row: Cast off 7, K6 (7sts)
- Turn the work:

BODY – LEFT SIDE

RIGHT SIDE FACING:
- 1st row: K7 from back leg, cast on 9, K5 from front leg (21sts)
- 2nd row: K
- 3rd row: K19, inc in next, K1 (22sts)
- 4th row: K1, inc in next, K20 (23sts)
- K 8 rows
- 13th row: K1, K2tog, K20 (22sts)
- 14th row: K19, K2tog, K1 (21sts)
- 15th row: K1, K2tog, K18 (20sts)
- 16th row: K17, K2tog, K1 (19sts)
- 17th row: K4 – put onto pin, cast off

9, K5 (6sts)
- Put 6 sts on pin.

BACK LEG – RIGHT SIDE

Work as back leg – left for 13 rows
- 14th row: K7, cast off 7

FRONT LEG – RIGHT SIDE

Work as front leg left for 11 rows
- 12th row: cast off 5, K5
- 13th row: K5
- Turn the work

BODY – RIGHT SIDE

RIGHT SIDE FACING:
- 1st row: K5 from front leg, cast on 9, K9 from back leg (21sts)
- 2nd row: K
- 3rd row: K1, inc in next, K to end (22sts)
- 4th row: K20, inc in next, K1 (23sts)
- K 8 rows
- 13th row: K20, K2tog, K1 (22sts)
- 14th row: K1, K2tog, K19 (21sts)
- 15th row: K18, K2tog, K1 (20sts)
- 16th row: K1, K2tog, K17 (19sts)
- 17th row: K6 – put on pin, cast off 9, K3 (4sts)

TAIL

With wrong side facing
- 1st row: K4 from right side, K4 from left side (8sts)
- 2nd row: K3, K2tog, K3 (7sts)
- K 2 rows
- 5th row: K2tog, K3, K2tog (5sts)
- K 5 rows
- 11th row: K2tog, K1, K2tog (3sts)
- K 2 rows
- 14th row: K3tog – pull wool through

HEAD

Knitting from neck to nose
With right side facing
- Put 6sts from left side, and 6sts from right side onto needle (12sts)
- 1st row: K12
- 2nd row: sl 2, K8 – turn –
- 3rd row: K8, K2tog
- 4th row: K4, inc in next 2sts, K3, K2tog (12sts)
- 5th row: K12
- 6th row: sl 2, K3, inc in next 2sts, K3 – turn –
- 7th row: K10, sl 2 (8sts)
- 8th row: K2, inc in next, K1, inc in next, K4, inc in next, K1, inc in next, K2 (18sts)
- 9th row: K15 – turn –
- 10th row: K12 – turn –
- 11th row: K12 – turn –
- 12th row: K12 – turn –
- 13th row: K15
- 14th row: K2 – put onto pin, K16 (16sts)
- 15th row: K2 – put onto pin as above, K14 (14sts)
- 16th row: K4, inc in next, K4, inc in next, K4 (16sts)
- 17th row: K4, inc in next, K6, inc in next, K4 (18sts)
- K 2 rows
- 20th row: K4, inc in next 2sts, K6, inc in next 2sts, K4 (22sts)
- K 3 rows
- 24th row: inc in 1st, K5, K2tog, K2tog, K2, K2tog, K2tog, K5, inc in last (20sts)
- 25th row: K7, K2tog, K2, K2tog, K7 (18sts)
- 26th row: K
- 27th row: K2, K2tog, K1, K2tog, K4, K2tog, K1, K2tog, K2 (14sts)
- 28th row: K
- 29th row: K1, K2tog, K1, K2tog, K2, K2tog, K1, K2tog, K1(10sts)

- 30th row: K
- Cast off

BODY GUSSET

- Take 4 sts from under chin
- K 2 rows
- 3rd row: K1, inc in next, K2 (5sts)
- K 50 rows
- 54th row: K2, K2tog, K1(4sts)
- K 2 rows
- 57th row: K1, K2tog, K1 (3sts)
- K 2 rows
- 60th row: K3 tog – pull wool through
-

EARS – MAKE TWO

Size 10/3.25mm needles

- Cast on 8
- K 3 rows
- 4th row: K2, K2tog, K2tog, K2 (6sts)
- 5th row: K
- 6th row: K1, K2tog, K2tog, K1 (4sts)
- 7th row: K
- 8th row: K1, K2tog, K1(3sts)
- 9th row: K
- 10th row: K3tog – pull wool through

To make up:
Sew up back leg seams & stuff.
Sew up centre backbone, neck to tail.
Sew up tail from tip to half-way towards top of legs.
Sew up under chin – stuff head.
Sew gusset to left and right sides through stomach – leave gap for stuffing.
Stuff and finish sewing up.
To give definition, trim down hair with small scissors taking care not to cut into knitting – the hair is thicker on lower body, legs and muzzle; shorter on tail, upper body and upper head.
Stitch ears to top of head so that they

sit high and pert, and just touching in the middle.
Add character to your dog with well-placed black beads for eyes and nose. Use black embroidery thread around the nose for added definition.
Add eyebrows by taking 20cm length of wool, folding over on itself a few times – stitch together and secure over eyes. Add ribbon at neck.

Woof!

MATERIALS:
Colour Codes:
1 Rowan Kidsilk Haze
(shades 00649 & 00658) –
knitted together
2 Rowan Baby Merino Silk DK Shell
Pink (for nose)
Beads (for eyes)

Embroidery thread in Yellow & Green
6mm diameter × 1m dowel
Craft/florist wire
Stuffing

NEEDLES:
Size 10/3.25mm
Size 10/3.25mm double-ended
Crochet hook

Highland Cattle

H ighland cattle have their place amongst Scotland's most iconic things. With their shaggy coat, messy ginger fringe over their eyes and long horns, they are well adapted to surviving the bitter Scottish winter and whatever Atlantic gales happen to be blowing through. Not being picky eaters also helps them thrive where other breeds would struggle, and they can make productive use of land that would otherwise be useless. With their rugged nature and excellent meat, Highland cattle have been exported around the world but it is their handsome appearance in the landscape of the Highlands that makes them a Scottish favourite.

Work in reverse stocking stitch.

BACK LEFT LEG

COLOUR 1 – THE TWO SHADES KNITTED TOGETHER

- Cast on 11
- 1st row: K

- 2nd row: P
- 3rd row: K3, K2tog, K1, K2tog, K3 (9sts)
- 4th row: P
- 5th row: K2, K2tog, K1, K2tog, K2 (7sts)
- 6th row: P
- 7th row: K1, K2tog, K1, K2tog, K1 (5sts)
- 8th row: P
- 9th row: K
- 10th row: P
- 11th row: Inc 1st & last (7sts)
- 12th row: P
- 13th row: Inc 1st and last st (9sts)
- 14th row: P
- 15th row: Inc in 1st, K2, inc in next, K1, inc in next, K2, inc in last (13sts)
- 16th row: P
- 17th row: Inc in 1st, K3, inc in next, K3, inc in next, K3, inc in last (17sts)
- 18th row: P
- 19th row: Inc in 1st, K4, inc in next, K5, inc in next, K4, inc in last (21sts)
- 20th row: P
- 21st row: Cast off 10, K to end

Put on a pin to set aside

FRONT LEFT LEG

CAST ON 11 – COLOUR 1, BOTH SHADES TOGETHER

Work as back left leg until row 17
- 18th row: Cast off 8, K8   (9sts)

BODY – LEFT SIDE

- Take front left leg section with RS facing (i.e.: reverse side of stocking stitch)
- Cast on 5
- 1st row: P (14sts)
- 2nd row: Cast on 2, K to end (16sts)
- 3rd row: Cast on 5, P to end (21sts)
- 4th row: K21, K11 (from set aside pin of back left leg) (32sts)
- 5th row: Cast on 2 (34sts)
- Work 14 rows of SS
- 19th row: P1, P2tog, P to end
- 20th row: K to last 3, K2tog, K1
- 21st row: P, cast off all BUT 7, P to end
- 22nd row: K
- 23rd row: P, cast off 2, P to end
- Cast off remaining sts

BACK RIGHT LEG

Work same as back left leg up to row 20
21st row: K11, cast off 10 (11sts) – set aside on pin as before

FRONT RIGHT LEG

- Work as front left leg up to row 17
- 18th row: K9, cast off 8 (9sts)
-
BODY – RIGHT SIDE

- Take front right leg section with right side facing (i.e.: reverse side of stocking stitch)
- Cast on 2
- 1st row: P to end   (11sts)
- 2nd row: Cast on 5, K to end (16sts)
- 3rd row: P
- 4th row: Cast on 5, K to end (21sts)
- 5th row: P21, P11 (from set aside pin of back right leg), cast on 2 (34sts)

- Work 14 rows SS
- 20th row: K1, K2tog, K to end
- 21st row: P to last 3, P2tog, P1
- 22nd row: Cast off all BUT 7sts, K to end   (7sts)
- 23rd row: P to end
- 24th row: Cast off 2, K5
- Cast off

HEAD – STARTING WITH NOSE

COLOUR 2

- Cast on 5
- Work 6 rows in GS
- Change to double-ended & Colour 1 (work two main shades together)
- 7th row: Needle 1 – K5
- Needle 2 – Picking up 3sts on short side of square
- Needle 3 – Picking up 5sts on bottom edge of square
- Needle 4 – Picking up 3sts on remaining side of square
- Work 4 rows K
- 12th row: Needle 1 – Inc in 1st & last (7sts)
- Needle 2 – K3
- Needle 3 – K5
- Needle 4 – K3
- 13th row: Needle 1 – Inc in 1st & last (9sts)
- Needle 2 – K3
- Needle 3 – Inc in 1st & last (7sts)
- Needle 4 – K3
- 14th row: Needle 1 – Inc in 1st, K3, inc in next, K3, inc in last   (12sts)
- Needle 2 – Inc in 1st, K2 (4sts)
- Needle 3 – K7
- Needle 4 – K2, inc in las   (4sts)
- 15th row: Needle 1 – Inc in 1st, K4, inc in next, K5, inc in last (15sts)
- Needle 2 – Inc in 1st, K2, inc in last (6sts)

- Needle 3 – K7
- Needle 4 – As Needle 2
- Work 4 rows K
- 20th row: P
- 21st row: Needle 1 – P1, P2tog, P9, P2tog, P1 (13sts)
- Needle 2 – P6
- Needle 3 – P7
- Needle 4 – P6
- Work 3 rows P
- 25th row: Needle 1 – P (13sts)
- Needle 2 – P5, last st put on Needle 3
- Needle 3 – P8, plus P1 from Needle 4 (9sts) and put on pin
- 26th row: Starting on Needle 4 – work as SS backwards and forwards P to end
- 27th row: K to end (23sts)
- 28th row: Cast off 2, P2tog, P14, P2tog, P2 (19sts)
- 29th row: Cast off 2, K2tog, K12, K2tog (15sts)
- 30th row: Cast off 2, P12 (13sts)
- 31st row: Cast off 2, K10 (11sts)
- Cast off

BELLY GUSSET

- From Needle 3 – Take 9sts and work 14cm in SS (i.e.: reverse side of stocking stitch)
- 1st row: K2tog, K2tog, K1, K2tog, K2tog (5sts)
- 2nd row: P
- 3rd row: K2tog, K1, K2tog (3sts)
- 4th row: P
- 5th row: K3tog
- Pull wool through

EARS – MAKE TWO

- Cast on 3
- 1st row: K
- 2nd row: P
- 3rd row: Inc 1st & last (5sts)
- 4th row: P
- 5th row. K
- 6th row: P
- 7th row: Inc 1st & last (7sts)
- 8th row: P
- 9th row. K
- Cast off

To make up: Sew up leg seams and stuff. Join body sections at centre spine, from neck to tail. Inset gusset through tummy, leaving middle section open for stuffing. Sew on head. Stuff and sew up at tummy section. Attach ears to head. Attach beads as eyes. Using crochet hook, knot in shaggy fringe. For the horns use whatever comes to mind – a crafted shape of cardboard, pipe cleaner, craft wire, twig – push through head and secure as necessary.

You will need

MATERIALS:
Colour Codes:
1 Debbie Bliss Baby Cashmerino
Black
2 King Cole Cuddles Chunky White

Black lightweight cotton covered
millinery wire
Black beads
Stuffing

NEEDLES:
Size 10/3.25mm
Size 10/3.25mm double-ended
Jewellery pliers

Sheep

Sheep and Scotland go hand-in-hand – or hand-in-woolly-glove in the winter. A number of popular breeds have been farmed in Scotland over the centuries, from the older traditional breeds like Soay Sheep from St Kilda and Shetland Sheep to the two most popular breeds of today, the Cheviot and the Blackface. The Scottish Borders are now the centre of sheep farming, although sheep played an important part in the Highland Clearances of the eighteenth and nineteenth centuries, when landowners realised that sheep would make them more money than people and the agricultural revolution forced mass emigration from the land, with many heading off to North America and Australasia.

A sheep called Dolly was also the first mammal in the world to be successfully cloned, at the Roslin Institute near Edinburgh. She lived for six years and her preserved remains are now a permanent exhibit at the National Museum of Scotland and a lasting reminder of the most famous sheep in the world.

BODY

Size 10/3.25mm
COLOUR 2
- Cast on 22
- Work 22 rows in GS
- Next row: K4, K2tog, K2, K2tog, K2, K2tog, K2, K2tog, K4 (18sts)
- Next row: K3, K2tog, K1, K2tog, K2, K2tog, K1, K2tog, K3 (14sts)
- Next row: cast off 6, K1, slip 2 right-hand stitches onto pin to make i-cord tail, cast off 6
- Re-join thread to 2 centre sts – work 12 rows of i-cord to make tail
- K2tog, pull-through last st

HEAD

Size 10/3.25mm double-ended
COLOUR 1
- Cast on 6
- 1st row: P
- 2nd row: inc in 1st, K5, inc in next (8sts)
- 3rd row: P
- 4th row: inc in 1st, K2, inc in next, inc in next, K2, inc in last   (12sts)
- Divide onto 3 needles – 4sts each needle.
- 5th row: K to join the needles
- 6th row: Needle 1 – K2, inc in next, K1 (5sts)
- Needle 2 – inc in 1st, K2, inc in last (6sts)
- Needle 3 – K1, inc in next, K2 (5sts)
- 7th row: K
- 8th row: Needle 1 – K3, inc in next, K (6sts)
- Needle 2 – inc in 1st, K4, inc in last (8sts)
- Needle 3 – K1, inc in next, K1 (6sts)
- Work 8 rows
- Cast off

LEGS

Size 10/3.25mm double-ended
COLOUR 1
- Cast on 8sts
- 1st row: K
- 2nd row: P
- 3rd row: K
- 4th row: P1, P2tog, P2tog, P2tog, P1 (5sts)
- 5th row: K2tog, K1, K2tog (3sts)

Using 3 sts as i-cord, work 7 rows for front legs/8 rows for back legs
K3tog & pull through last st

EARS

Size 10/3.25mm
COLOUR 1
- Cast on 3
- 1st row: K
- 2nd row: P
- 3rd row: K1, inc in next, K1 (4sts)
- 4th row: P
- 5th row: K1, inc in next, K2 (5sts)
- 6th row: P
- 7th row: K
- 8th row: P
- 9th row: K
- 10th row: P
- 11th row: K2tog, K1, K2tog (3sts)
- 12th row: P
- Cast off

To make up:
Join body, leaving neck-edge open. Stuff. Join head, leaving neck-edge open. Stuff. Pin neck-edge of head to opening in body – think 'sheep' – adjust as necessary and stitch on.

Attach ears to head. Dampen with water and tweak into sympathetic shape with fingers. They will hold this shape when dry.

Cut two pieces 25cm long of black lightweight cotton covered millinery wire. Bend into U-shape – these will be the front and legs. Poke wire down left front leg using jewellery pliers, turn end of wire to create ball for hoof. Push wire through body to repeat process for right front leg. Match leg lengths, create ball for hoof and snip off wire. Stitch up hoofs around wire ball.

Repeat process for back legs. Kink out back legs to give character, as they are not straight like the front legs.
Add black beads for eyes. Wind orange/red thread around base of beads for detail.

(Tip: Reinforce with extra stitching where the wire joins the body to give stability for standing.)

One sheep ready for the mountainside!

Saltire

MATERIALS:
Colour Codes:
1 Sirdar Country Style Blue
(shade 0476)
2 Sirdar Calico DK White

NEEDLES:
Size 10/3.25mm

Small Thistle

MATERIALS:
Colour Codes:
1 Rowan Felted Tweed Green
(shade 158)
2 Sirdar Super Soft Aran Purple
(shade 0900)

NEEDLES:
Size 10/3.25mm double-ended
Size 12/2.75mm for the leaf

The Saltire

The Saltire is the national flag of Scotland. It is also known as the St Andrew's Cross after St Andrew, the patron saint of Scotland, who was crucified on a cross turned on its side as he felt unworthy of crucifixion on the same upright cross as Jesus. St Andrew was adopted as Scotland's patron saint around 1,000 years ago, possibly during the reign of William I, although it is likely that the flag dates back to the time of Oengus II in the ninth century, who led his force of Picts and Scots against the invading Angles led by Athelstan.

Legend has it that in his prayers before battle, Oengus vowed that if he was victorious then he would appoint St Andrew as patron saint. The next morning, before the battle, a white cross appeared in the blue sky, which Oengus and his troops took as a good omen. When battle was joined, a famous victory was won against the odds and the Saltire flag was born.

Now, the National Flag Heritage Centre is situated in the village of Athelstaneford in East Lothian, the village having been named after Athelstan, who was slain nearby as he retreated from the battle against Oengus II and his army. The writer Nigel Tranter was an enthusiastic supporter of the Scottish Flag Trust and was instrumental in setting up the National Flag Heritage Centre to celebrate the story of the Saltire.

We recommend using two separate balls of white until row 19, and from row 27. Work in SS with blue & white wool used in each row.

COLOURS 1 AND 2 NEEDED, ALTERNATING AS INDICATED BELOW

- Cast on 48
- K 2 rows to create border
- *K 2sts in blue at beginning and end of every row to create side border*
- Pattern within the blue border:
- 1st row: K4 white, K36 blue, K4 white
- 2nd row: P5 white, P34 blue, P5 white
- 3rd row: K6 white, K32 blue, K6 white
- 4th row: P7 white, P30 blue, P7 white
- 5th row: K1 blue, K7 white, K28 blue, K7 white, K1 blue
- 6th row: P2 blue, P7 white, P26 blue, P7 white, P2 blue
- 7th row: K3 blue, K7 white, K24 blue, K7 white, K3 blue
- 8th row: P4 blue, P7 white, P22 blue, P7 white, P4 blue
- 9th row: K5 blue, K7 white, K20 blue, K7 white, K5 blue
- 10th row: P6 blue, P7 white, P18 blue, P7 white, P6 blue
- 11th row: K7 blue, K7 white, K16 blue, K7 white, K7 blue
- 12th row: P8 blue, P7 white, P14 blue, P7 white, P8 blue
- 13th row: K9 blue, K7 white, K12 blue, K7 white, K9 blue
- 14th row: P10 blue, P7 white, P10 blue, P7 white, P10 blue
- 15th row: K11 blue, K7 white, K8 blue, K7 white, K11 blue
- 16th row: P12 blue, P7 white, P6 blue, P7 white, P12 blue
- 17th row: K13 blue, K7 white, K4 blue, K7 white, K13 blue
- 18th row: P14 blue, P7 white, P2 blue, P7 white, P14 blue
- 19th row: K15 blue, K14 white, K15 blue
- 20th row: P16 blue, P12 white, P16 blue
- 21st row: K17 blue, K10 white, K17 blue
- 22nd row: P18 blue, P8 white, P18 blue
- This is half-way.
- 23rd row: K18 blue, K8 white, K18 blue
- 24th row: P17 blue, P10 white, P17 blue
- 25th row: K16 blue, K12 white, K16 blue
- 26th row: P15 blue, P14 white, P15 blue
- 27th row: K14 blue, K7 white, K2 blue, K7 white, K14 blue
- 28th row: P13 blue, P7 white, P4 blue, P7 white, P13 blue
- 29th row: K12 blue, K7 white, K6 blue, K7 white, K12 blue
- 30th row: P11 blue, P7 white, P8 blue, P7 white, P11 blue
- 31st row: K10 blue, K7 white, K10 blue, K7 white, K10 blue
- 32nd row: P9 blue, P7 white, P12 blue, P7 white, P9 blue

- 33rd row: K8 blue, K7 white, K14 blue, K7 white, K8 blue
- 34th row: P7 blue, P7 white, P16 blue, P7 white, P7 blue
- 35th row: K6 blue, K7 white, K18 blue, K7 white, K6 blue
- 36th row: P5 blue, P7 white, P20 blue, P7 white, P5 blue
- 37th row: K4 blue, K7 white, K22 blue, K7 white, K4 blue
- 38th row: P3 blue, P7 white, P24 blue, P7 white, P3 blue
- 39th row: K2 blue, K7 white, K26 blue, K7 white, K2 blue
- 40th row: P1 blue, P7 white, P28 blue, P7 white, P1 blue
- 41st row: K7 white, K30 blue, K7 white
- 42nd row: P6 white, P32 blue, P6 white
- 43rd row: K5 white, K34 blue, K5 white
- 44th row: P4 white, P36 blue, P4 white

- K 2 rows in blue
- Cast off
- Darn ends

Use flag as decorative panel for a bag, cushion, wall-hanging – creative opportunities are endless, limited only by your imagination!

Small Thistle (to use as keyring/zip-pull)

Using Colour 1 starting with the bulb, work from the top to the stem

- Cast on 12
- 1st row: K
- 2nd row: (K1, P1, inc in next, P1, K1, inc in next) repeat (16sts)
- 3rd row: (K1 P1) repeat to end
- 4th row: (K3, inc in next) repeat to end (20sts)
- 5th row: (K2, P1) repeat 6 times, K2
- 6th row: (K4, inc in next) repeat to end (24sts)
- 7th row: K1, (P1, K2) repeat 7 times, P1, K1
- 8th row: (K3, inc in next) repeat to end (30sts)
- 9th row: (K1, P1) repeat to end
- 10th row: K1, (P1, K2) repeat 9 times, P1, K1
- 11th row: (P1, K1, P1, K2tog) repeat to end (24sts)
- 12th row: (K1, P1, K2tog) repeat to end (18sts)
- 13th row: (K2tog, P2tog) repeat to last 2st, K2tog (9sts)
- 14th row: (K2tog, P2tog) repeat to last st, K1 (5sts)
- 15th row: K2tog, K3 (4sts)
- Work as 4 st i-cord for 4cm
- K2tog, K2tog, pull wool through

LEAF

COLOUR 1

Needle: Size 12/2.75mm

Worked from the tip to the stalk

- Cast on 3
- 1st row: P
- 2nd row: K row – inc in middle st (4sts)
- 3rd row: K1, P2, K1
- 4th row: K1, inc in next 2 st, K1 (6sts)
- 5th row: K1, P4, K1
- 6th row: K
- 7th row: K1, P4, K1
- 8th row: K4, inc in next 2 st (8sts)
- 9th row: K1, P6. K1
- 10th row: K6. inc in next 2 st (10sts)
- 11th row: K2tog, cast off 2, P5, inc in last st (7sts)
- 12th row: Cast on 1, then inc in this and next st, K6 (10sts)

- 13th row: K2tog, P7, K1 (9sts)
- 14th row: K row – inc in 1st, K8 (10sts)
- 15th row: K1, P8, K1
- 16th row: K2tog, cast off 3, K5 (6sts)
- 17th row: K1, P3, K2tog (5sts)
- 18th row: K2tog, K3 (4sts)
- 19th row: K1, P1, K2tog (3sts)
- 20th row: K2tog, K1 (2sts)
- Pull wool through
- Use this end to sew leaf onto stalk.

To make up:

Sew up side of thistle bulb.

With purple wool (Colour 2) wind strands around card about 5cm wide and tie into a bundle, push into top opening of thistle and secure with a few stitches. Trim purple fluff if necessary.

Attach leaf to stalk.

Sew the end of the stalk onto a keyring or zip-pull.

You will need

MATERIALS:
Colour Codes:
1 Debbie Bliss Baby Cashmerino
Black
2 Cream DK
3 Rowan Fine Lace (Blue shade
00933) – use double
4 Rowan Fine Lace (Red shade
00935) – use double
5 Sublime Cashmere Merino Silk DK
(Yellow shade 0250)
6 Rowan Cotton Glaze
(Green shade 812)

Embroidery thread in Yellow & Green
6mm diameter x 1m dowel
Craft/florist wire
Stuffing

NEEDLES:
Size 10/3.25mm
Size 11/3.00mm
Size 10/3.25mm double-ended

Bagpipes

W hat could be more Scottish than the skirl of the bagpipes? Although there have been many similar instruments around the world, it is the Great Highland Bagpipe that is now known worldwide through its use in the military and in pipe bands. Bagpipes first arrived in Scotland around 1400 and are now most commonly played in pipe bands or solo pibrochs. Such was the symbolic power of the bagpipes that it is said they were banned after the Battle of Culloden in a bid to weaken the morale of the Scots. Later, however, when Scottish soldiers played an integral part in the expansion of the British Empire, they took their bagpipes around the globe, on occasion terrifying the locals with the mighty sound. Today, bagpipes are as popular as ever, from a solo piper at a wedding to traditional pipe bands at the Highland Games to The Red Hot Chilli Pipers, who have brought jock'n'roll bagpipes to a whole new generation.

BLOWSTICK

COLOUR I
Size 10/3.25mm
- Cast on 6
- 1st row: K
- 2nd row: P
- 3rd row: K row – inc in every st (12sts)
- Work 11 rows in GS
- 15th row: (K2tog) repeat to end (6sts)
- Work 19 rows in SS starting with P
- 35th row: K row – inc in every st (12sts)
- Work 5 rows in GS
- Work 8 rows SS starting with P row
- 50th row: (P2tog) repeat to end (3sts)
- 51st row: K
- 52nd row: P
- Pull wool through 3 sts
- Use thread to start sewing up

To make up: Sew item around 10cm length of dowel. Insert stuffing into wider sections.

TENOR DRONES – MAKE TWO

COLOUR I
Size 10/3.25mm
- Cast on 6
- 1st row: K
- 2nd row: P
- 3rd row: K row – inc in every st (12sts)
- Work 11 rows GS
- 15th row: K row – inc in every st (24sts)
- 16th row. Join Colour 2 – P row
- 17th row: K
- 18th row: P
- 19th row: P
- 20th row: P
- 21st row: (K2tog) repeat to end (12sts)
- 22nd row: Join Colour 1– (P2tog) repeat to end (6sts)
- Work 14 rows ss starting with K row
- 37th row: K row – inc in every st (12sts)
- 38th row: P
- 39th row: Join Colour 2 – K row – inc in every st (24sts)
- 40th row: P
- 41st row: K
- 42nd row: K
- 43rd row: K
- 44th row: P
- 45th row: K
- 46th row: (K2tog) repeat to end (12sts)
- 47th row: Join Colour 1 – K row
- Work 15 rows GS
- 63rd row: (K2tog) repeat to end (6sts)
- Work 17 rows SS starting with P
- 81st row: K row – inc in every st (12 sts)
- 82nd row: P
- 83rd row: Join Colour 2 – K row – inc in every st (24 sts)
- 84th row: P
- 85th row: K row – inc in every stitch (48sts)
- 86th row: K
- 87th row: (K2tog) repeat to end (24sts)
- 88th row: (P2tog) repeat to end (12sts)
- 89th row: (K2tog) repeat to end (6sts)
- Pull wool through all 6 sts

To make up: Sew item around 16cm length of dowel. Insert stuffing to wider sections.

BASE DRONE

COLOUR I
Size 10/3.25mm
- Cast on 6
- 1st row. K
- 2nd row: P
- 3rd row: K row – inc in every st (12sts)
- Work 13 rows GS
- 17th row: K row – inc in every st (24sts)
- 18th row: Join Colour 2 – Pl
- 19th row: K
- 20th row: P
- 21st row: K
- 22nd row: K
- 23rd row: (K2tog) repeat to end (12sts)
- 24th row: Join Colour 1 – (P2tog) repeat to end
- Work 14 rows SS starting with K row
- 39th row: K row – inc in every st (12sts)
- 40th row: P
- 41st row: Join Colour 2 – K row – inc in every st (24sts)
- Work 6 rows SS starting with P
- 48th row: (P2tog) repeat to end (12sts)
- 49th row: Join Colour 1 – K row
- Work 16 rows GS
- 66th row: (P2tog) repeat to end (6sts)
- Work 18 rows: SS starting with K
- 85th row: K row – inc in every st (12sts)
- 86th row: P
- 87th row: Join Colour 2 – K row – inc in every st (24sts)
- 88th row: P
- 89th row: K
- 90th row: K
- 91st row: K
- 92nd row: P

- 93rd row: K
- 94th row: (P2tog) repeat to end (12sts)
- 95th row: Join Colour 1 – K row
- Work 22 rows GS
- 118th row: P2tog (6 sts)
- Work 20 rows SS starting with K
- 139th row: K row – inc in every st (12sts)
- 140th row: P
- 141st row: Join Colour 2 – K row – inc in every st (24sts)
- 142nd row: P
- 143rd row: K row – inc in every st (48sts)
- 144th row: K
- 145th row: (K2tog) to end (24sts)
- 146th row: (P2tog) to end (12sts)
- 147th row: (K2tog) to end (6sts)
- Pull wool through all 6 sts

To make up: Sew item round 27cm length of dowel. Insert stuffing to wider sections.

CHANTER

COLOUR 1
Size 10/3.25mm
- Cast on 6
- 1st Row: K
- 2nd row: P
- 3rd row: K
- 4th row: P
- 5th row: K row – inc in every st (12sts)
- Work 11 rows GS
- 17th row: (K2tog) repeat to end (6sts)
- Work 33 rows SS starting with P
- 51st row: Join Colour 2 – K row – inc in every st (12sts)
- 52nd row: P
- 53rd row: K row – inc in every st (24sts)

- 54th row: P
- 55th row: K row – inc in every st (48sts)
- 56th row: P
- 57th row: K
- 58th row: K
- 59th row: K
- 60th row: (P2tog) repeat to end (24sts)
- 61st row: K
- 62nd row: P
- 63rd row: (K2tog) repeat to end (12sts)
- 64th row: P
- 65th row: (K2tog) repeat to end (6sts)
- 66th row: (P2tog) repeat to end (3sts)
- Pull wool through

To make up: Sew item around 12cm length of dowel. Insert card circle to widest section – approx. 4.5cm diameter. Insert stuffing to both wider sections.

TARTAN BAG

COLOUR 3, COLOUR 4, COLOUR 5 NEEDED
Size 11/3.00mm
Cast on 75
- 1st row: K34, turn –
- 2nd row: P34
- 3rd row: K49, turn –
- 4th row: P4 in blue, (P6 in red, P3 in blue) 4 times, turn –
- 5th row: (K3 in blue, K6 in red) 4 times, K9 in blue, turn –
- 6th row: P9 in blue (P6 in red, P3 in blue) 5 times
- 7th row: (K3 in blue, K6 in red) 5 times, K30 in blue
- 8th row: P30 in blue (P6 in red, P3 in blue) 5 times

- 9th row: (K3 in blue, K6 in red) 5 times, K1 in blue, turn –
- 10th row: P46 in blue
- 11th row: K75 in yellow
- 12th row: P60 in blue, turn –
- 13th row: K3 in red (K3 in blue, K6 in red) 6 times, K3 in blue
- 14th row: (P3 in blue, P6 in red) 8 times, P3 in blue
- 15th row: K yellow wool to end (75sts)
- 16th row: (P3 in blue, P6 in red) 8 times, P3 in blue
- 17th row: (K3 in blue, K6 in red) 4 times, K3 in blue, K4 in red, turn –
- 18th row: P4 in red (P3 in blue, P6 in red) 4 times, P3 in blue
- 19th row. K75 in blue
- 20th row: P75 in yellow
- 21st row: K75 in blue
- 22nd row: (P3 in blue, P6 in red) 8 times, P3 in blue
- 23rd row: (K3 in blue, K6 in red) 8 times, K3 in blue
- 24th row: (P3 in blue, P6 in red) 8 times, P3 in blue
- 25th row: (K3 in blue, K6 in red) 4 times, K1 in blue, turn –
- 26th row: P1 in blue, (P6 in red, P3 in blue) 4 times
- 27th row: (K3 in blue, K6 in red) 8 times, K3 in blue
- 28th row: P75 in blue
- 29th row: K75 in yellow
- 30th row: P75 in blue
- 31st row: (K3 in blue, K6 in red) 8 times, K3 in blue
- 32nd row: (P3 in blue, P6 in red) 8 times, P3 in blue
- 33rd row: (K3 in blue, K6 in red) 8 times, K3 in blue
- 34th row: P75 in yellow
- 35th row: (K3 in blue, K6 in red) 8 times, K3 in blue

- 36th row: (P3 in blue, P6 in red) 8 times, P3 in blue
- 37th row: K75 in blue
- 38th row: P75 in yellow
- 39th row: K75 in blue
- 40th row: (P3 in blue, P6 in red) 8 times, P3 in blue
- 41st row: (K3 in blue, K6 in red) 8 times, K3 in blue
- 42nd row: (P3 in blue, P6 in red) 8 times, P3 in blue
- 43rd row: (K3 in blue, K6 in red) 8 times, K3 in blue
- 44th row: (P3 in blue, P6 in red) 8 times, P3 in blue
- 45th row: (K3 in blue, K6 in red) 8 times, K3 in blue
- 46th row: P75 in blue
- 47th row: K75 in yellow
- 48th row: P75 in blue
- 49th row: (K3 in blue, K6 in red) 4 times, K1 in blue, turn –
- 50th row: P1 in blue (P6 in red, P3 in blue) 4 times
- 51st row: (K3 in blue, K6 in red) 8 times, K3 in blue
- 52nd row: P75 in yellow
- 53rd row: (K3 in blue, K6 in red) 8 times, K3 in blue
- 54th row: (P3 in blue, P6 in red) 8 times, P3 in blue
- 55th row: K75 in blue
- 56th row: P75 in yellow
- 57th row: K75 in blue
- 58th row: (P3 in blue, P6 in red) 8 times, P3 in blue
- 59th row: (K3 in blue, K6 in red) 4 times, K3 in blue, K4 in red, turn –
- 60th row: P4 in red, (P3 in blue, P6 in red) x4, P3 in blue
- 61st row: (K3 in blue, K6 in red) 8 times, K3 in blue
- 62nd row: (P3 in blue, P6 in red) 8 times, P3 in blue

- 63rd row: (K3 in blue, K6 in red) 8 times, K3 in blue
- 64th row: P60 in blue and turn
- 65th row: K 60 in yellow
- 66th row: P75 in blue
- 67th row: (K3 in blue, K6 in red) 5 times, K1 in blue, turn –
- 68th row: P1 in blue, (P6 in red, P3 in blue) 5 times
- 69th row: K75 in yellow
- 70th row: P cast off 21 in blue, P8 in blue (P6 in red, P3 in blue) 5 times
- 71st row: (K3 in blue, K6 in red) 5 times, K9 in blue
- 72nd row: P cast off 5 in blue, P3 in blue, (P6 in red, P3 in blue) 4 times, turn –
- 73rd row: K40 in blue
- 74th row: P cast off 15 in blue, P33 in blue
- 75th row: K34 in blue
- 76th row: P cast off 34 in blue

To make up:
Embroider yellow lines vertically through centre of alternative red squares.

Embroider green lines vertically through centre of every blue line.

Embroider green horizontally alongside every knitted yellow row.

FRINGED BANDS – ON EACH OF THREE DRONES, BLOWSTICK & CHANTER
COLOUR 4
Size 11/3.00mm
- Cast on 20
- Work 15 rows SS
- Cast off

(use folded in half)

FRINGED BAND – FOR END OF BAG
Colour 4
Size 11/3.00mm
- Cast on 27
- Work 5 rows SS
- Cast off

FRINGE
Take a piece of card 30cm x 5cm. Cut a letterbox slot in the centre 13cm x 0.5cm. Wind red wool around the narrow width of the card covering the slot in a single layer. Using a very small stitch or stretch stitch on a sewing machine, sew through the length of the letterbox slot. Cut the edges of wool to create double-edged fringe. Sew onto the knitted bands above for each pipe and end of bag. Cut the fringe to desired length.

DRONE CORDS WITH TASSELS
Work two lengths of 3 stitch i-cord in red on double-ended needles, one 80cm long, one 10cm long. Make a tassel for each end of both cords. Knot the long cord around the three drones and the short cord around the top of the bass drone.

To make up:
Sew the piece of tartan into a tube, leaving the back end open.
Wind a piece of wire around bottom end of each pipe. Insert through knitted bag in correct position as bagpipe design. Secure in place by twisting wire around a length of dowel used as a 'rail' on the inside of the bag. Wind a piece of wire around the top end of the Chanter and thread through end of knitted bag as per

bagpipe design. Secure pipe in place by drawing bag tight around the dowel. Sew a fringed band around the base of each pipe and catch to the surface of the bag to cover the join. Stuff the bag. Insert fringed piece to end of bag before finally sewing up.

You will need

MATERIALS:
Colour Codes:
1 Rowan Sienna Grey
2 3X Anchor Lame Silver metallic
embroidery thread
3 2X Anchor Lame Red metallic
embroidery thread

Piece of stiff card
Stuffing

NEEDLES:
Size 10/3.25mm

Chocolate Teacake

Many countries around the world have chocolate-coated marshmallow treats. The first such treat is credited to the Danes in the early nineteenth century and there are examples in the USA, Germany, Holland, Scandinavia, Portugal, Peru, Russia, Australia and in many other countries. However, the iconic teacake made by Tunnock's in Scotland must surely be one of the finest there is and it's now exported around the globe. With its round biscuit base and a delicious dome of soft marshmallow on top, all fully coated in milk chocolate – or dark chocolate if you prefer – the Tunnock's Teacake is a delicious treat at any time of the day.

DOMED TOP OF CAKE

COLOUR 1 AND COLOUR 2 KNITTED TOGETHER

- Cast on 40
- Work 9 rows SS starting with P row
- 10th row: K3, K2tog, (K6, K2tog) 4 times, K3 (35sts)
- 11th row: P
- 12th row: K2, K2tog, (K4, K2tog) 5 times, K1 (29sts)
- 13th row: (P2, P2tog) 7 times, P1 (22sts)
- 14th row: (K2, K2tog) 5 times, K2 (17sts)
- 15th row: P
- 16th row: (K2, K2tog) 4 times, K1 (13sts)
- 17th row: (P1, P2tog) 4 times, P1 (9sts)
- 18th row: (K2tog) 4 times, K1 (5sts)

Cut thread, tie off last stitch. Thread a length of wool through 5 stitches, pull up tightly and tie off.

BASE

COLOUR 1 AND COLOUR 2 KNITTED TOGETHER

- Cast on 10
- Work in SS
- 1st row: P
- 2nd row: K inc in 1st & last (12sts)
- 3rd row: P
- 4th row: K inc in 1st & last (14sts)
- 5th row: P
- 6th row: K inc in 1st & last (16sts)
- Work 6 rows SS starting with P
- 13th row: P2tog, P12, P2tog (14sts)
- 14th row: K
- 15th row: P2tog, P10, P2tog (12sts)
- 16th row: K
- 17th row: P2 tog, P8 (10sts)
- 18th row: K
- Cast off

To make up:

Buy a real chocolate teacake (we recommend Tunnock's) to use as reference.

Join sides of domed top piece. Over-stuff very firmly – stuffing should spill out until base is attached. Press and mould to shape.

Cut circle of card 60mm diameter. Place over bottom of teacake to retain stuffing. Stretch knitted base over cardboard. Sew edges of base to top section.

Take length of silver thread and work a running stitch around teacake a little way up from the base – tighten gently as you work to create the lip edge of the biscuit base. Secure once circle is complete.

To decorate as per foil wrapper, take red metallic thread, embroider star at centre top and two concentric red circles. Stitch perpendicular red metallic lines (Colour 3) in slightly irregular fashion like crumpled foil around the teacake, crossing under the base and reaching 2.5cm up the sides.

To finish – put the kettle on, unwrap the real teacake, sit back and admire your handiwork.

You will need

MATERIALS:
Colour Codes:
1 Gedifra Aneja
(Copper shade 01121)
2 Rowan Fine Milk Cotton
(Pale Green shade 482)
3 Debbie Bliss Baby Cashmerino
Black

Water-based stiffener
Sheet of clear Acetate approx.
25cm x 15cm
Stuffing

NEEDLES:
Size 10/3.25mm double-ended

Scotch Whisky

Scotch whisky, or *uisge beatha* (water of life) in Gaelic, is one of the finest drinks in the world and a major Scottish export. There is a vast range on offer, from single malts to blended Scotch whisky, each with its own distinctive characteristics. Traditionally, whisky was produced in pot stills, although modern techniques of continuous distillation are now almost universal.

Scotland is divided into distinct whisky regions, each with their own distilleries, with Speyside the most numerous and including famous names such as Glenfiddich, The Glenlivet, The Macallan and Balvenie. There are also distilleries in the Highlands, including Glenmorangie and Old Pulteney, in the Islands, in Campbeltown and in Islay. Such is the demand for whisky around the world that exports are now valued at more than £4bn and the industry directly employs more than 10,000 people in Scotland. Brazil is currently the world's fastest growing market for whisky, with Singapore and Taiwan not far behind.

And for any whisky lover, a visit to the distillery is all part of the experience, and Speyside's Malt Whisky Trail, to the east of Inverness, is a great way to spend a few days, especially if someone else is doing the driving.

BOTTLE

COLOUR 1

- Cast on 48
- Divide between 3 needles – make into circle
- Work 75 rows
- 76th row: (K2, K2tog) repeat to end (36 sts)
- 77th row: K
- 78th row: (K2, K2tog) repeat to end (27 sts)
- 79th row: K
- 80th row: (K1, K2tog) repeat to end (18 sts)
- Work 6 rows
- 87th row: Join Colour 2, work 8 rows
- 96th row: (K1, K2tog) repeat to end (12 sts)
- 97th row: K
- 98th row: Join Colour 3, inc in every other st (18 sts)
- 99th row: K
- 100th row: P
- 101st row: K
- 102nd row: P
- Work 6 rows
- 109th row: P
- 110th row: K
- 111th row: P
- 112th row: P
- 113th row: (K2tog, K1) repeat to end (12 sts)
- 114th row: K
- 115th row: (K2tog) repeat to end (6sts)
- 116th row: K2tog (3 sts)
- Pull wool through

BOTTLE BASE

COLOUR 1

- Cast on 8 on 4 double-ended needles – 2sts per needle – make into circle
- 1st row: K

- 2nd row: inc in every st (16 sts)
- Work 3 rows
- 6th row: inc in every st (32 sts)
- Work 5 rows
- 12th row: inc in every stitch (64 sts)
- 13th row: K
- Cast off

BOTTLE LABEL

COLOUR 2

- Cast on 26
- Work 21 rows in SS – on P rows K1st & last st
- Cast off Knit-wise

To make up:
Create a tube with the acetate rectangle. Insert into the bottle piece up to the neck shaping. Stuff the whole bottle, including the bottle neck.
Sew bottle base in place.
Embroider label and sew onto bottle.

WHISKY TUMBLER

COLOUR 2

- Cast on 8 onto 4 needles – 2sts per needle – make into circle
- 1st row: K
- 2nd row: (yf, K1) repeat to end (16 sts)
- Work 3 rows
- 6th row: (yf, K1), repeat to end (32 sts)
- Work 5 rows
- 12th row: (yo, P1) repeat to end (64 sts)
- 13th row: P
- 14th row: K
- 15th row: (P1, P2tog) repeat to end (43 sts)
- 16th row: K
- 17th row: K
- 18th row: K1, (yf, sl 1, K1, psso, K1,

K2tog, yf, K1) repeat to end
- 19th row: K
- 20th row: K1, (fy, K1, sl 1, K2tog, psso, K1, yf, K1) repeat to end
- 21st row: K
- 22nd row: K1, (K2tog, yf, K1, yf, sl 1, K1, psso, K1) repeat to end
- 23rd row: K
- 24th row: K2tog, (K1, yf, K1, yf, K1, sl1, K2tog, psso) repeat to last 5 st, K1, yf, K1, yf, K1, ssk
- 25th row: K
- 26th row: K1, (yf, sl 1, K1, psso, K1, K2tog, yf, K1) repeat to end
- 27th row: K
- 28th row: K1, (fy, K1, sl 1, K2tog, psso, K1, yf, K1) repeat to end
- 29th row: K
- 30th row: K row – inc every 7th st, K1 (49 sts)
- 31st row: K
- 32nd row: K row – inc every 5th st (59 sts)
- Work 10 rows K
- Cast off loosely

To make up:
Darn ends. Using water-based stiffener soak knitted glass completely. Remove and blot dry. Shape using hairdryer, tweaking and coaxing all the way. When dry enough to form a believable glass shape, leave overnight to dry completely. Add your whisky in the morning!

WHISKY-COLOURED INSERT

COLOUR 1

- Cast on 8 on 4 needles – make into circle
- 1st row: K
- 2nd row: K row – inc in every st (16 sts)

- Work 3 rows
- 6th row: K row – inc in every st (32 sts)
- Work 5 rows
- 12th row: K row – inc in every st (64 sts)
- 13th row: K
- 14th row: K
- 15th row: P
- 16th row: (K1, K2tog) repeat to end, K1 (43 sts)
- Work 9 rows
- Cast off

To make up: Cut a disc of foam 1cm depth to fit inside knitted insert. Place inside bottom of tumbler.

You will need

MATERIALS:
Colour Codes:
1 Cotton Mix 'Pastry'-Coloured DK
2 Grey/Pink Boucle-Textured DK

Stuffing
12cm sq. piece of 1cm thickness foam

NEEDLES:
Size 10/3.25mm
Size 10/3.25 double-ended
3.25mm crochet hook

Scotch Pie

Local delicacies and different foods help define who we are, and you can't beat a good Scotch pie. This little jewel of a pie has a double crust for extra texture and is filled with delicious minced mutton. Ideal as a snack or served with mash and beans, it's also to be found as a half-time treat at football grounds around the country. The meat is usually nice and peppery and the hot water crust pastry keeps it all neatly packed together and adds a bit of crunch to the pie. And in the depths of a Scottish winter, a hot Scotch pie can taste very good indeed.

BASE

COLOUR I

Crochet 8 stitches – arrange on 4 needles – knit with 5th needle:

- 1st row: K
- 2nd row: inc in every stitch (16sts)
- 3rd, 4th, 5th row: K
- 6th row: inc in every stitch (32sts)
- Work 5 rows K
- 12th row: inc in every stitch (64sts)
- Work 7 rows K
- 20th row: inc in every stitch (128sts)
- 21st row: K
- 22nd row: (K2tog, K1) repeat to end (84sts)
- Work 2 rows K
- 25th row: (K4, K2tog, K9, K2tog, K4) 4 times (76sts)
- Work 2 rows K
- 28th row: (K4, K2tog, K7, K2tog, K4) 4 times (68sts)
- Work 2 rows K
- 31st row: (K4, inc in next, K7, inc in next, K4) 4 times (76sts)
- 32nd row: K

Cast off knitting into back of stitch – leave long tail of wool. Thread onto needle and weave through finished edge. This gives a better, thicker finished pie edge.

LID

COLOUR I

- Cast on 14
- 1st row: K
- 2nd row: P row inc 1st & last
- Repeat 1st & 2nd rows 4 times (24sts)
- Work 4 rows SS
- To create hole in pie:
- 15th row: K3, cast off 3, K17 (18sts)
- 16th row: P16, P2tog
- Slip 3 separate stitches onto double-ended needle
- 17th row: K row – inc in 1st, K16 (18sts)
- Cut thread – slip stitches onto double-ended needle
- With right side facing, join yarn to the 3 stitches:
- 18th row: K2, inc in next, turn –
- 19th row: P4
- 20th row: Work full row with both sets of stitches: K3, inc in next, K1, inc in next, K16 (24sts)
- 21st row: P2 tog, P20, P2tog (22sts)
- 22nd row: K
- 23rd row: P2tog, P18, P2tog (20sts)
- 24th row: K
- 25th row: P2tog, P16, P2tog (18sts)
- 26th row: K
- 27th row: P2tog, P14, P2tog (16sts)
- 28th row: K2tog, K12, K2tog (14sts)
- Cast off

FILLING

COLOUR 2

- Cast on 6
- Work in GS
- 1st row: K
- 2nd row: inc in 1st & last (8sts)
- Repeat 1st & 2nd rows to 20sts
- Work 4 rows
- Cast off

To make up:
Cut circle of foam to fit base of pie. Add 3 or 4 pieces of wadding to give an even surface. Place the semi-circle of filling on top of wadding and catch to sides of pie. Place pie lid on top. The hole in lid should be positioned to fit over the semi-circle of filling. Catch with stitches. Colour creatively with brown pastel pencils, as if baked in a hot oven.

Appendix: Basic Doll

MATERIALS
Colour Codes:
1 Rowan Baby Merino Silk DK Shell Pink

Stuffing

NEEDLES
Size 10/3.25mm

ARMS – SHOULDER TO WRIST

- Cast on 5
- 1st row: K to end
- 2nd row: P to end
- 3rd row: K row – inc in 1st & last (7sts)
- 4th row: P to end
- 5th row: K row – inc in 1st & last (9sts)
- 6th row: P to end
- Work 24 rows

TO CREATE LEFT HAND

- 31st row: K2, put 2 on pin, K5
- 32nd row: P to end bringing 2 sections together   (7sts)
- 33rd row: K
- 34th row: P
- 35th row: K2tog, K2tog, K2tog, K1
- 36th row: P2tog, P2tog
- Pull thread through

TO CREATE RIGHT HAND

- 31st row: K5, put 2 on pin, K2 (7sts)
- 32nd row: P
- 33rd row: K
- 34th row: P
- 35th row: K1, K2tog, K2tog, K2tog

- 36th row: P2tog, P2tog
- Pull thread through

THUMB – SAME FOR BOTH HANDS

- Put 2sts from pin on double-ended needle
- Join thread, K2
- K2tog as i-cord
- Pull thread through

To make up: Join seams. Stuff.

LEGS

- Cast on 20
- 1st row: P
- 2nd row: K
- 3rd row: P
- 4th row: K6, K2tog, K1, K2tog, K1, K2tog, K6 (17sts)
- 5th row: P
- 6th row: K4, cast off 9, K3 (8sts)
- 7th row: P, pulling 2 sections of 4 together
- Work 4 rows SS starting with K
- 12th row: K1, inc in next, K4, inc in next, K1 (10sts)
- Work 7 rows SS starting with P
- 20th row: K1, inc in next, K6, inc in next, K1 (12sts)
- Work7 rows SS starting with P
- 28th row: K1, inc in next, K8, inc in next, K1 (14sts)
- Work 15 rows SS starting with P
- Cast off

To make up: Join seam. Pull top of foot together. Stuff

BODY – FRONT

- Cast on 16
- 1st row: K
- 2nd row: P
- 3rd row: K1, inc in next, K12, inc in next, K1 (18sts)
- Work 3 rows SS starting with P
- 7th row: K1, K2tog, K2, K2tog, K4, K2tog, K2, K2tog, K1   (14sts)
- Work 3 rows SS starting with P
- 11th row: K2, inc in next, K8, inc in next, K2   (16sts)
- 12th row: P
- 13th row: Inc in 1st, K3, inc in next, K6, inc in next, K3, inc in last (20sts)
- Work 5 rows SS starting with P
- 19th row: K1, sll, K1, psso, K14, K2tog, K (18sts)
- Work 3 rows SS starting with P
- 23rd row: K1, sll, K1, psso, K12, K2tog, K1 (16sts)
- 24th row: P1, P2tog, P10, P2tog, P1 (14sts)
- 25th row: K1, sll, K1, psso, K8, K2tog, K1 (12sts)
- 26th row: P
- Cast off

Notes